What Readers Say

"This was such an uplifting book, and I felt Archangel Michael was with me whilst I was reading it. I recommend this book to anyone who is going through their own personal awakening." A.H.

"I am so deeply touched by the love and compassion that enfolds me when I read Archangel Michael's messages. They are so full of understanding without judgment for our human condition, and show the way to upliftment without prerequisite." M.W.

"An 'eye and heart opening' experience, to say the least. At last, I understand that all our trials and tests have purpose and meaning, and that it is time to move into a state of grace, leaving the wheel of karma, or cause and effect, behind." D.B.

"It puts me on an 'angelic high.' I have experienced the full gambit of bliss, euphoria, sadness and hope as beloved Archangel Michael helps us to remember who we are, where we are from and our mission here on Planet Earth." S.W.

"I urge all that are guided to this book to savor and re-read it over and over until all the wonderful jewels of wisdom are absorbed and integrated. Ronna's wonderful gift to this Earth Plane is her channeling work with Archangel Michael. This book is the first in a series to come that shares Archangel Michael's messages for our journey and spiritual path.

"We are so dearly loved. The Angelic realm has been trying to tell us this for many years. I wish you good reading and the love of Archangel Michael."

Carolyn Ann ORiley, The Archangel's Pen
www.carolynannoriley.com

More Reader Comments

"Archangel Michael as brought forth by Ronna Herman reminds us all of our own power, purpose and divinity. His words empower us to access our true source of wisdom within and to couple that with our divine right use of will. This powerful combination allows us to walk the middle path of balance toward our certain fulfillment as physicalized spiritual beings. Through Archangel Michael's simple but profound teachings, we are able to receive guidance for ourselves as well as offer support, devotion and dedication to others at times when our own words and deeds would otherwise fail us.

"Ronna has walked her talk longer than anyone I know. She has been and continues to be my mentor simply by being a living example of the art form of truth and integrity. No other author or channel has touched me as deeply.

"Ronna's presence in my life has lovingly coaxed and evoked the best in me to emerge and to make itself known to others. I am eternally grateful and hold her in highest esteem."

Pepper Lewis, Channel for Mother Earth (Gaia),
Author of *Gaia's Voice, Mother Earth Speaks from the Heart*
www.thepeacefulplanet.com

"*On Wings of Light* contains a wealth of information, wisdom and spiritual insight. A gift of great value to everyone."

Arnold Zimmerman
Author of *Butterflies of Light and Voices of Nature*

"Archangel Michael's teachings have been a constant inspiration and source of spiritual wisdom in my life since Ronna Herman first became his messenger. *On Wings of Light* is truly filled with the love and Light of Archangel Michael."

Rev. Paula McIntyre, La Mesa, California

On Wings of Light

Messages of Hope and Inspiration

From Archangel Michael

Through Ronna Herman
A Cosmic Telepath

Mt. Shasta Light Publishing

On Wings of Light

2nd Edition

ISBN: 0-9700902-3-4

Published by:

Mt. Shasta Light Publishing
P. O. Box 1509
Mt. Shasta, CA 96067-1509 USA

Phone: 530.926.4599

Fax: 530.926.4159

Email: aurelia@mslpublishing.com

Website: www.mslpublishing.com

Ronna Herman may be contacted at:

StarQuest
6005 Clear Creek Drive
Reno, NV 89502 USA

Phone/Fax: 775.856.3654

Email: ronnastar@earthlink.net

Web site: www.ronnastar.com

I invite you to take a journey with me, a journey into the unseen realms where angels dwell. Put your analytical mind aside, if you will, and feel with your heart and inner knowing. Allow the words to resonate and see if they do not touch a chord of truth deep within, a memory of times long past when we communed and walked with the angels.

I present Archangel Michael's messages to you in the form they were given to me, with little editing or grammatical corrections. The messages have a flavor, a style; he uses words in a way that may not be acceptable in literary circles, but they resonate with his essence of love and compassion, and therefore, I bring them to you in the same way.

When I am ready to channel a message, I sit before my computer and surround myself with white Light and call on my Beloved I AM Presence. I feel my consciousness lift until it connects with Archangel Michael's energy as it gently moves down through my crown chakra until the message comes forth. The words tumble out very quickly, in almost perfect copy (a typo once in a while). I can channel a message in forty-five minutes to an hour, sometimes a little longer (depending on the complexity of the information). I am conscious as I channel, an observer of the process, somewhat separated, but aware.

I have a wonderful, constant connection with Lord Michael's energy, I feel his presence overshadow me, day and night. This blessing has transformed my life and expanded my consciousness beyond my wildest imagining. Many of us have followed parallel paths with the angelic forces down through the ages: interacting, assisting, creating, learning as we soared throughout the universe. We are returning to our natural state where we will hear, see and walk with the angels and the Ascended Masters, no longer able to deny our divinity.

Lord Michael states that his words are infused with the Essence of Love and Light transmitted through him from the God/Goddess/Creator. Allow this energy to permeate your Being as you feel the warmth of his Presence.

The messages are not always in the order he gave them to me. He determined the sequence in which they would be presented in this book. However, they seem to have taken on an even richer, fuller meaning, I think, because we are wiser and more able to fully understand what he has been trying to convey to us these past few years in his loving, patient way.

I offer this gift to you in the same manner it was given to me.

With Love, Ronna

Credits:

On Wings of Light was lovingly edited by an angel friend: Barbara Herbert of Reno, Nevada. Book design and formatting was done by Aaron of Mt. Shasta Light Publishing.

Front cover photo of Archangel Michael by Peggy Black: "Sacred Sound Salutarist" guided by angelic realms, the essence of Kuan Yin, and the energy and presence of the Hathors. A world traveler and lecturer, she conducts workshops and retreats for women. She is passionate about sharing the incredible wonders of the "Sacred Sounds" as a healing modality. She is a creative artist with a line of angel greeting cards and a series of "Angel Montages" photographs. Phone: 831.335.3145, Address: 661 Felton Empire Road, Felton, CA 95018, Website: www.healingmusic.org/PeggyBlack.htm, Email: peggyblack@aol.com

Back cover photo of Inter-Dimensional Portal Opening at Grimes Point, Nevada, by Cher Price, Sparks, Nevada.

Contents

1. Love of Life

L is for LOVE,

I is for INFINITE,

F is for FULL OF IT,

E is for EVER.

Life has a beginning, it has an end,

And in between you can begin

To grow and learn or coast and drift,

Meet the challenge, help and lift

Your spirits up, and those around,

Give a hand, take a hand, understand.

Feel it...live it...give it all you've got;

Be the best you can, forget what you are not.

Don't waste it; fill it with laughter, sprinkle with tears,

And when you come to the end of your years

You can look back and proudly say,

This time around, I gave life its full play.

I travelled along life's spiral road,

I reached the top

And enjoyed the trip all the way.

Ronna Herman

2. The Beginning

I would like to give you a brief background of my life so that you will know that I am no different than you. We all have the ability to commune with the angels and higher beings; it is our birthright, we have just forgotten. Archangel Michael, other angelic beings, and the Ascended Masters are making themselves known to greater and greater numbers of people every day. The veil between dimensions is thinning and we are breaking through the illusion of separation from the God Force. Communing with these beautiful beings is the norm; the abnormal was when we were cut off and could no longer interact with our Higher Selves and the Messengers of the GOD/GODDESS/CREATOR OF ALL.

More and more people are speaking of their paranormal experiences, some of which are breathtaking in their beauty and others are uncomfortable, confusing and disconcerting. All are part of the transformational process we have been experiencing for the last twenty or so years.

In telling my story, it might help you and those you know to understand what is happening when you begin to experience clairaudience, (clear hearing), clairvoyance (clear seeing), visions, multidimensional realities, out-of-body experiences, flashes of past lives and deja vu. I feel it is important that I share the transitions I have gone through, my spiritual awakening and quest that finally culminated in my becoming a cosmic telepath and messenger of ARCHANGEL MICHAEL.

Although I have always been a seeker of truth and, even at a very young age, was frustrated and discontent with the fundamentalist religion my parents forced on me, it was not until I was forty years old that I began to get some answers and realize there was something "out there" much vaster than I had been taught.

At that time, I was administrative assistant to the president of a television equipment manufacturing firm in Salt Lake City. I had recently married Kent Herman, who was the Regional Marketing Director for Western Airlines (second time around for both of us). We took wonderful vacations all over the world, flying to exotic places I never imagined I would have the opportunity to visit. We loved our work, each other and had a satisfying, exciting life together. A lovely lady named Vickey was head of the advertising department where I worked and she and I became close friends. She was powerful and wise, far beyond her years, and way ahead of her time. One day, she came into my office and told me about an interesting workshop she had attended the evening before in which one of the things they talked about was automatic writing, what it was and how to accomplish it.

She proceeded to show me what to do and after holding the pencil in my hand for a few minutes, without any conscious help on my part, my hand began to make swirls and squiggles and then began to write; "Lilliam Beemer, Lilliam Beemer." As she had been taught, she told me to ask if it was permissible for me to know what this meant. The reply was, "Not at this time." I then wrote, or my hand wrote, "Go to your typewriter." I did so, resting my hands lightly on the keyboard and almost immediately my hands began to fly over the keys. The message went something like this, "We are glad to make contact with you at last. You are to be a transmitter of a new awareness, a higher truth. One of your purposes is to become a writer and you will be given information to impart to those who are ready to listen. But first there will be an awakening and a cleansing and testing period." There

was more but this is basically the content of the message.

Vickey stood by, amazed, and after I had stopped typing and she read the message, she exclaimed, "Wow! That came too easily; you have certainly done this before in another lifetime. I think we should not go any further with this until we educate you a little and teach you how to protect yourself."

And so it began. I had read a little about Eastern religions and reincarnation, but did not think much about it one way or another. I guess I thought it was as plausible as what I had been taught in Sunday School as a child, but up to that time, I had not read or heard anything that resonated in my heart as my truth.

The first book Vickey brought me to read was Edgar Cayce's life story, There Is A River, and it literally blew my belief system to pieces. The Seth material by Jane Roberts opened up more vistas for my consciousness and shattered many of my superstitions and structured beliefs. It left me feeling vulnerable and alone. It was difficult to learn that there was not a GOD "out there" who was pulling strings and controlling our lives, that we were responsible for our own reality and "IT" was all up to us.

It was as if I were obsessed. I began to read every metaphysical book I could find. I went to a dentist who used hypnosis to relax his patients and found I could slip into an altered state almost immediately. He told me, "You are one of the best subjects I have ever had." I asked him if he could recommend any books on the subject. He did, and shortly after I read the first one, my husband, his sixteen year old son, Dan, and I went on a rafting trip down the Colorado River. It was a thrilling, exciting trip and we were having a marvelous time until the third day. As we were executing one of the

most difficult rapids on the river, the front left pontoon was torn loose and folded back over the front of the boat where I was sitting, twisting my left leg up and back, breaking it in three places. There was a spiral fracture of the tibia and the fibula had snapped in two places.

I was flown out by helicopter and after the orthopedic surgeon in Salt Lake City had finished setting the bones and put the cast on he told me, "You will probably be in this full cast for at least three months. Bones take a lot longer to heal at your age."

I spent much of my time in my husband's big, comfortable recliner, reading and practicing self-hypnosis. I found that I could take the pain away for as long as forty-five minutes at a time. After a few days I threw away the pain pills. I began to concentrate on sending healing energy to my leg and visualizing it strong and well. After six weeks, when my husband, Kent, was taking me to the doctor for x-rays, I told him, "I am going to get a walking cast today."

He said, "Don't get your hopes up, honey; it's too soon."

When the doctor came into the room after looking at the x-rays, he said, "This is amazing; your leg has healed as well and quickly as that of a sixteen year old. I think we can put on a walking cast today."

Kent was flabbergasted!

I said to the doctor, "Don't laugh at me, but I would like to tell you what I have been doing."

After I finished my story, he replied, "I'm not laughing; it worked. There is so much about the brain and mind power that we are just beginning to realize and investigate.

Whatever you are doing, keep it up. It certainly won't hurt."

I was out of the walking cast in three months and skiing in five months. My leg never atrophied and has never given me a minute of pain.

I began to study more about reincarnation and altered states of consciousness and was soon meditating on a regular basis. Before long, I began to have flashes of past lives. I am not a visionary. I do not see pictures; there was just a knowing. The story would unfold in my mind and I would feel things that had happened. I learned that Lilliam Beemer was my name in a very important past life. It answered a lot of questions, including the reason for my sad, unfilled relationship with my father. In my book Once Upon a New World, *the section entitled "The Warrior Maid" is based on that lifetime. It did not happen often, but every now and again a lifetime would come into my consciousness and I would realize or learn how it affected my current relationships, and was the basis of many of my fears and impulses.*

My husband was transferred to San Diego in 1976. The move was quite traumatic for us at the time, but I later realized it was all part of the divine plan. I acquired my real estate broker's license and got a position managing an office of thirty to thirty-five people. I met another wonderful teacher and was soon deeply involved in astrology and later began to give spiritual astrology readings.

By this time, I was channeling regularly on my typewriter and had begun to do past life readings for my family and friends. I would sit with my hands lightly on the typewriter, ask a question about a relationship or a problem and soon a story or explanation would roll out. At times, I would sing or recite poetry to be sure the information was not coming from

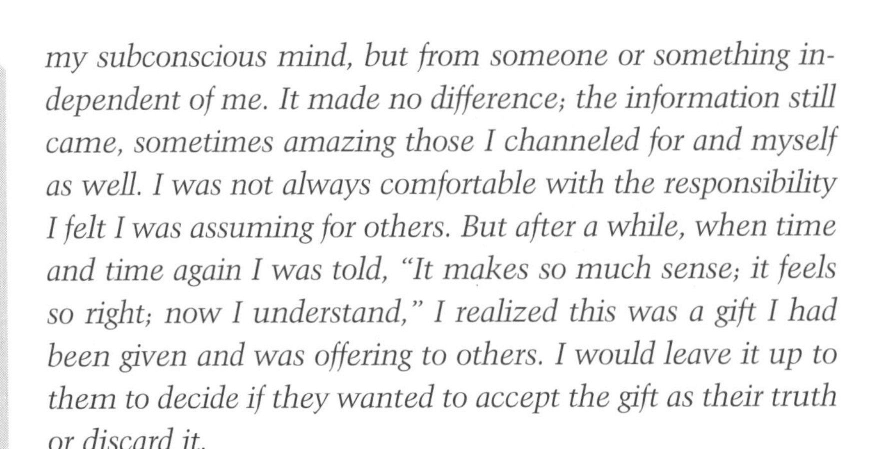

my subconscious mind, but from someone or something independent of me. It made no difference; the information still came, sometimes amazing those I channeled for and myself as well. I was not always comfortable with the responsibility I felt I was assuming for others. But after a while, when time and time again I was told, "It makes so much sense; it feels so right; now I understand," I realized this was a gift I had been given and was offering to others. I would leave it up to them to decide if they wanted to accept the gift as their truth or discard it.

I was channeling several different guides on my typewriter by that time; the one who most often came through called himself Anthony and he told me he was one of my personal guides. I also channeled a gentle, loving entity who called herself Al-E-Ta.

In 1984, both my husband and I retired. We had worked long and hard during our careers, travelled extensively, and enjoyed all the social scene had to offer. We agreed that what we wanted most was to enjoy the serenity, peace and quiet of our beautiful Alpine home. Through another set of circumstances that I now realize was also divine intervention, we were led to buy the home, situated on one and a third acres, with towering oaks and a lovely little stream flowing through it. It is a story in itself, but will suffice to say it was a miracle that led us to the property, and miraculous the way all obstacles melted away so that we could dispose of two other properties and close the transaction in the thirty days allotted.

I now had the time to devote to my studies, reconnect with mother earth while planning the landscaping for our yard and enjoy retirement with my husband. It all seemed perfect, and

then in 1986 the cleansing process really began. I developed bronchial pneumonia which left me weak and debilitated. I began to gain weight and have back problems. I was miserable and disillusioned.

I meditated; I prayed and often asked, "Why...why now, when I am trying so hard to live my spiritual beliefs? What am I doing wrong?"

This continued until early springtime, 1987. I remember the day so clearly. I had just finished doing some yoga exercises and was stretched out on the floor to meditate. I felt so despondent and sad, as if life or all I had done had no meaning. My eyes were tightly closed, but the tears poured out and ran down my face. I felt as if I were a tiny dot of energy floating out in the vastness of space...in my mind's eye, I held my soul in my hands, and lifting them up toward God, I said, "I don't know what to do. Here, you take it, you must know what to do with it."

All of a sudden, as if there were a megaphone in my ear, I heard this deep voice say, loud and clear, "Well, it's about time; we've been waiting for you to get your ego out of the way so we can begin to work with you. We are called TRITON, and we will be your teacher henceforth."

For a while, I thought I must be going insane, as day after day, while working out in the yard or doing my housework, I carried on this conversation in my head, asking questions about everything imaginable, and always receiving a clear, concise, loving answer. I asked about all my relationships, events in my life and their meanings. I also wanted to know about my most important past lives, who the characters were then, and what role they played in my current life. My feelings of frustration and sadness over different experiences and

failures disappeared as all the puzzles and pieces of my life seemed to fall into place and everything began to make such perfect sense.

I told my story to some of my closest friends and family, those who I knew would understand and not be shocked. Soon I was asking questions for them and relaying answers, and before long TRI-TON began to encourage me to allow him to use my voice. Again, I was frightened and hesitant, working only with those closest to me—those with whom I felt completely loved and safe. Soon, I was doing past life regressions with TRI-TON lovingly directing and guiding my clients, helping them to experience the emotions and reality of those important relationships and lifetimes, breaking boundaries, clearing negative thought-forms.

My health improved and I began to see the world in a whole new light. It seemed as if I floated through the days, doing whatever needed to be done, whether digging in the yard, cleaning house or being absorbed in my spiritual work. It was as if part of me was an observer in that wonderful perfect place, while my body performed all the physical tasks.

By this time, many of my friends were going through the cleansing and clearing process, growing by leaps and bounds. We felt the need to share what we were learning and experiencing, to give support and encouragement. We began to meet every other week and share information, books and what we were learning at seminars and workshops. We studied together, meditated together and created a warm, loving spiritual family unit that is intact today, although many have gone in different directions and taken a different spiritual path.

We all were expanding and growing rapidly in our spiritual awareness. Time was speeding up and the world was

changing at a dizzying pace. I was channeling TRI-TON on a regular basis, both in private sessions and group sessions. I often channeled at our group meetings, and everyone in the group could feel his loving, dynamic energy when he was speaking through me.

He told us that he was part of a vaster energy, an essence of many parts, a multidimensional being (not really a he, of course), but the energy felt strong and masculine. He always said "we" and told us that this unit of energy had never incarnated in the physical but had always been a teacher from the Higher Causal and Mental Planes in the world of the etheric. The energy was a part of our vaster "Oversoul" and we, who had come together to learn and grow, reuniting as a soul family here on earth, would one day be reunited with this vast being, bringing our awareness, love and experience to add to the whole. He said he was available to any of us once we broke through the energy veil of accumulated negative thought and emotional vibrations. Soon, many of our group were getting answers or impulses from TRI-TON, and felt a very close connection to this loving entity.

One day, when I was working in the yard, I had just started toward our small grove of Christmas trees to trim the new growth when TRI-TON said, "It is time for you to begin to write. You will write a book and it will be entitled *"Once Upon a New World." I was somewhat taken aback, but having no idea what this book was to be about, and how I could accomplish such a task, I did not give it much thought for a few weeks. And then, suddenly, scenes began to come into my mind and I felt compelled to write them down. I sat in the living room with my husband in the evening, and while he watched television, night after night I wrote, sometimes in long hand and sometimes in shorthand, my hand flying*

over the pages of a yellow legal size note pad as the story began to unfold. The next day I would correct and transcribe on my typewriter what I had written the night before. (I did not have a computer at that time). I finished the first draft of the manuscript in four months. Rewriting, refining and completing it took much longer. I laboriously typed the original 326-page manuscript twice on my typewriter, and made numerous additions and deletions. Then through another miracle, I had the opportunity to buy a used computer, the software, including WordPerfect, the printer, etc. at a bargain price. My dear friend, Connie, who found it for me also taught me what I needed to know to become computer literate enough to use it properly. So I again typed the manuscript, this time on floppy discs.

During that time, I also began to write poetry. I would wake up in the night with words tumbling through my mind. I had to write them down immediately, or they would be lost by morning. During a six-month period, I wrote over twenty poems, and then they stopped coming. Occasionally, I find another one building in my mind, but not often. And if I try to write one without my muse, it is a disaster.

During this period, 1987 to 1991, I experienced many things, some of which were difficult to share even with my Soul group. Often during meditation, I would shake so violently, my body would rise off the bed or floor. I often felt waves of energy flowing up and down my body, leaving me weak and then exhilarated. In meditation, I was taken to distant places, temples and gathering places, where it seemed as if mass initiations were taking place. Once when I was sitting outdoors on my favorite rock, meditating during a full moon, a voice said to me, "Are you ready?" I mentally said, "Yes." I was asked this three times and each time, I said "Yes."

That was all, nothing more. I wasn't sure what I had agreed to, but in my heart I felt I had given the only answer.

Shortly after that another event happened that jarred my reality. I had been collecting and using crystals and stones like so many other New Agers. I had a favorite generator crystal, and also a smaller double-terminated crystal I used in meditation. My friend Sarah and I were at a swap meet one Sunday and I was looking for a small crystal for a friend. As we peered into a dusty showcase filled with old costume jewelry and other treasures, in the corner I spied a dirty, dim crystal about three inches long and one inch wide at the base. I asked to see it, and when I took it in my hand, a chill coursed through my arm and body. I asked the price and when the lady said nine dollars, I immediately said, "I'll take it."

It took several days of cleansing, soaking and exposing it to the Sun before the crystal began to feel right. I didn't know where it had been, but I knew its journey had been long and tumultuous. The crystal was now pure, clear and smooth, without a blemish. It was somewhat flat, rather than round, and the tip came to a fairly sharp point. It fit beautifully in my hand and I began to use it in my meditations as my affinity for it rapidly grew.

One day, I was deep in meditation, with the crystal in my right hand, when my hand began to tingle and grow very warm, suddenly words came into my mind, not the voice of TRI-TON, just a knowing. "I am called Excalibur. I am symbolic of the tip of the mighty sword of Archangel Michael. I stand for courage, truth and divine will. I have returned to you so that you may remember that you are one of his own, a part of his beloved Legion of Warriors."

I sat quietly for a long time, but it said no more. I was

excited and awed and did not quite know what to make of this latest development, but after this experience I felt the need to have the crystal with me at all times. I sleep with it on the night table beside me, and I carry it in a little velvet pouch in my purse. When I channel on the computer I put it next to my heart and I do not feel complete when I meditate without it.

A few weeks later, during one of my private conversations with TRI-TON, he told me, "Soon, a new teacher of greatness will come to you. You have completed the cleansing process and the energy between us is now pure and uninhibited. You have become one with our energy so that we are now in perfect union. We grow and evolve as you do and we, too, are ever reaching higher and beyond. We are a part of you and you are a part of us. This is the desired path of ascension, to reach your Higher Self, unite, and then reach higher to the next and then the next level, toward the Christ-consciousness, and then higher to the Living Presence of the I AM THAT I AM. There are many levels and dimensions within dimensions on the path to ascension, and each step made is a victory."

I was astounded, to say the least, but it seemed I had taken on a new awareness, a new dimension. Whereas previously I had to go through a meditative process into an altered state to connect with TRI-TON'S energy, now it seemed the energy was with me all the time; I could plug into it like changing a radio frequency, by shifting my mind. I began to see people and events differently. I was able to look upon the seemingly lowest and most despicable being—murderer, rapist, felon—with compassion. Not for what they were and had done, but for that Spark of the Divine within them. Events or things rarely bothered me; I felt all was happening for a

reason, for the highest and best good. I became more tolerant and nonjudgmental. I stopped having opinions on many issues, seeing good and validity in all sides. In essence, I became more loving.

My spiritual group had a wonderful three day retreat over the 11:11 activation and acceleration on January 11, 1992. TRI-TON was with us and we all felt closely connected and in tune with Spirit. We all came home with a new awareness, a feeling that something profound had taken place.

A few days later, I decided to make a tape using TRI-TON's energy to record what had transpired over the three days. Immediately upon settling myself down with the tape recorder on, I felt a surge of energy go through my body. It seemed to gather and impact at the base of my skull. In a very deep, and seemingly far away voice, I began to speak:

"Beloved daughter of Light, I bring you greetings from the Most High. I come to you now in order to express my feelings of joy at your accomplishments and in the progress that you have made in such a short span of time. I come to you through the energy of the entity that you know as TRI-TON. You, who have become a clear channel of Light, and have opened the energy waves making it possible for me to connect with you through the compatible energy of TRI-TON. I am the one known to you as Archangel Michael. I will send you an angelic messenger who will transmit information from me, and you are to take this information on your computer so that it can be easily disseminated to others. Know that you are loved greatly and are under my direct guidance and protection, as well as that of the Ascended Masters."

For two days afterward, I felt somewhat out of it. I did not have a headache, but my head felt greatly expanded as though

there was a lot of energy impacted at the base of my skull; however, this gradually diminished. After an adjustment period of a few months, Lord Michael began to come to me directly instead of through his messenger. Now, when I sit at my computer, surround myself in the invincible Light, and connect with my I AM Presence, I feel a surge of gentle, loving energy flow through me as my hands fly over the keyboard. The messages come quickly, in almost perfect copy, and I always feel exhilarated, yet calm and peaceful when I am through. I feel very blessed to be the recipient of so much loving energy and awareness. I know I am never alone, and that my life does have purpose. I am not afraid of the future, and I do not buy into the doom and gloom scenario. It has not always been easy, but I wouldn't have missed a moment of it for the world. And it is wonderful to know that the BEST IS YET TO COME!

Love and Light to all of you on the Path. May your journey be as exhilarating, wonderful and fulfilling as mine has been. One sweet day, we will all be reunited.

Ronna

3. Doom and Gloom or a Joyous New World—The Choice Is Yours

Greetings, dear ones; we come to you as an angelic messenger of Archangel Michael.

We wish to speak to you today about your future and the future of your world as you know it. Are you buying into the doom and gloom and the destruction scenario, or are you at peace in the knowledge that the Universal plan of the Creator is perfect? You will get what you expect, you know? You are in the throes of the dawning of a New Age; a birthing process, and the birth of something new is always uncomfortable, but quickly forgotten in the rapture and beauty of new life.

You who are the Light workers, the vanguard of the New Age and new awareness, have a responsibility to focus your energy on the beauty and perfectness of the process. In other words, you must neutralize the negative energy that is bombarding your world via the fear, depression and feelings of hopelessness of those who are not capable of absorbing the increased energy being infused on your planet. The dark side of humankind is being exposed; it will no longer be tolerated. For those who continue to operate in the outdated mode of animal-man via greed, violence, selfishness, mistrust and denial, it will indeed seem as if the world has gone mad and chaos reigns.

So, more important than ever, is your responsibility of building your inner power source and focusing this energy on balance, peace and harmony—first within yourself, then joining with your spiritual partners in creating a synergy so powerful it could offset the negative energy of thousands. This is possible for you have the power of the Masters working with you. The masses are separated and impacting

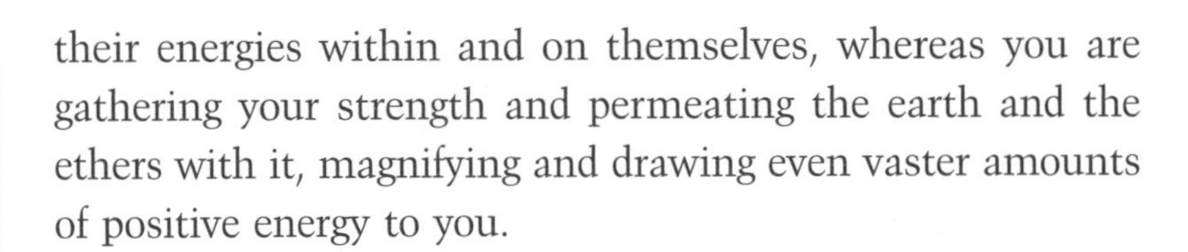

their energies within and on themselves, whereas you are gathering your strength and permeating the earth and the ethers with it, magnifying and drawing even vaster amounts of positive energy to you.

You are acting as an anchor for the mother earth as well; you are creating safe havens within the midst of turmoil. Do not allow fear or doubt to enter your consciousness. If you accept as fact all of the negative events predicted for your near future, this will indeed be your future. The more people who allow this kind of energy to enter their minds and then project it outwardly as their truth, the more likely these predictions are to become a reality. Remember, you are becoming co-creators within your own spiritual Master Self, along with creating all the positive affirmations you are expressing. If you do not discipline your thinking processes and especially your emotions at all times, there is a distinct possibility you will also manifest the cataclysmic events and dire predictions that are being circulated by well-meaning people.

Know you not that it is possible for the transformation to take place in a miraculous way, with a minimum of pain and destruction? Yes, the earth needs cleansing and, yes, the old ways of being and thinking must be transmuted, but you and those like you have been awakened and empowered just for the reason that you are capable of accomplishing these miracles.

We of other dimensions and realms are limited as to how much assistance we can give without the permission and acceptance of at least a portion of humankind. As you build your God-consciousness, you allow us to increase our assistance through you. We need you to realize your vast potential.

We encourage you to accept the universal truth that you are a co-creator with the God Force. What are your wildest dreams? What sort of world do you wish your earth to become? Build it in your mind, hold it in your heart and permeate your emotional nature with the yearning for it to manifest and then begin to affirm it into reality. All of the unmanifested energy of the Universe is at your disposal. Just reading and gaining knowledge is not enough. Just yearning and wishing is not enough. Know that you are gods-becoming. You must believe with all your being that you have an unlimited supply of all good things, all perfect things just waiting for you to claim them and bring them to fruition.

Dear ones, you must rise above what is thought to be good or bad. You must gather about you a cloak of neutrality, of nonjudgment. You must go forth in your awareness of perfect peace and harmony in attunement with your Higher Self and with your Christ-consciousness. Do not be swayed and do not feel you have to justify your beliefs or force your increased awareness on anyone. If one comes to you in need and asks for assistance and answers, indeed, supply what is needed. But remember the code of the Masters: dare to know, dare to do and be silent. Build your power within you, reinforce it through joint action and the loving energy of your spiritual family and go forth in all your dynamic glory and nothing can stop you from reaching your highest goal. It is assured.

More and more, each of you will become attuned to your own inner awareness, via intuition, telepathic messages or clairvoyance. If you stay centered and in control of your thought processes, you will always be informed as to what you should be doing or where you should be. YOU WILL ALWAYS BE IN THE RIGHT PLACE AT THE RIGHT TIME.

Our purpose is to give you encouragement and to assure you that your efforts are bearing fruit; you are making a difference. Can you not feel the difference in yourself? Enjoy the birth of your new awareness and the transformational process of your earth. Make it an exciting, exhilarating experience, a journey into new dimensions and the forerunner of paradise. The choice is yours. You have a saying, "The sky is the limit"; we tell you even the universe is not the limit. Know that you are loved and ever under the protection and guidance of Archangel Michael and the Masters.

4. The Process of Transformation

Question: Dear messenger, please explain why many of us are feeling so dizzy and weak and our sleep patterns are so erratic, i.e., need more sleep or at times hardly any sleep at all? Is it physical and, if so, what has caused it? Or, is it a spiritual process?

Yes, we come to you as an angelic messenger of Archangel Michael. Dear ones, we will explain to you the process that is now in progress and also what you should expect to take place in the immediate future. It is important that you all understand and do not become anxious or try to treat these symptoms with artificial means.

First of all, the process of transformation is being accelerated at a tremendous pace in order for you and other Light workers to be able to handle the incoming energies and to clear your bodily vehicles of residual negative energy. The reason for this is that any and all residual imbalance will create discomfort and also prevent you from accomplishing a complete transformation or transmutation. It is as if you are straddling two dimensions, dear ones; actually some of you are experiencing three dimensions at one time. Your physical being is operating in a world of the third dimension, your emotional and mental bodies are trying to adjust to the fourth-dimensional experience and your consciousness or Spirit Self is reaching for the fifth dimension, you see?

The molecular structure of your brain is redefining itself and also certain areas of your brain are being activated. Areas that have been in dormancy for thousands of years and also some critical areas that have not been active for millions of years. So you see, there is a reason for your discomfort, and distress. It is not physical in the sense you think of as

physical; in other words, you are not ill or there is no outside influence involved. The process is internal, cosmic and spiritual. Give yourself permission to rest when the discomfort occurs. When you feel the overwhelming urge to sleep, do so, for this is what is required. Listen carefully to the urgings and feelings of your physical vehicle, for it will speed up the process and make it easier and more comfortable for you.

Eat lightly, drink pure fluids, i.e., filtered water, fruit juices, fresh fruit and vegetables. All this will help to ease your discomfort. Please know and understand that your bodies will no longer be able to assimilate heavy, spicy, rich foods. Your internal and digestive system is being transformed or refining itself to the point that these foods will immediately result in a reaction of one sort or another. Some of you are already experiencing this and are wisely tuning in to the messages your are receiving.

Ordinarily, the process you and others are experiencing would happen over a period of several hundred years. Yes, we repeat, several hundred years, so you can see or imagine the shock and disorientation your physical vehicle is experiencing. Some of you are very distressed about the increase of bodily weight. Do not be; this has been necessary for those of you who will be making this monumental leap forward which will and has put a strain on your physical system. Your soul self is striving to bring all your bodily vehicles into balance and harmony as quickly as possible. Just as you have felt mental distress and confusion during your transitional period, now it is time for your physical body to follow. Your auric field is being cleared; you are bringing your mental, emotional and higher bodies into alignment, and just in time. The reports of a time shift and other manifestations are correct. Yes, the next phase is being put in place, the energies

are being increased, you are spiraling into the next higher rung of the evolutionary ladder. Part of the mechanics of this is that your earth's orbit is being lifted and the other part is that electromagnetic or cosmic energy bombardment is being increased tremendously. Expect more violence (the earth will absorb more and more energy also), as will all humans, animal and plant life. Those who are not equipped to handle this energy will become more violent, depressed, distressed and confused. Expect more suicides, more accidents, more unusual events—all part of the process, you see. You can imagine how powerful and invasive this energy is when you realize it penetrates to the center of the earth and everything and everyone on it. If it makes you dizzy and uncomfortable, how do you think it will make those poor unenlightened souls feel? More illness, mental and physical, more confusion, more hysterical outbreaks, and mental breakdowns. More violence among and toward each other—senseless acts of violence, people acting irrationally and unpredictably. Nothing that was dependable in the past will be dependable; old structures, religious and business, will fall by the wayside. If they are not infused with the light, they will not stand.

Your political process is on an emotional roller coaster. Much good will come from this, however. The masses are beginning to come out of their lethargy; they are beginning to question. The military is in the process of a complete mental and ethical overhaul. Your economy is stuck and the old ways of fixing it are not working. The Hierarchy has begun to take control of many areas which heretofore have been considered off limits. Here again, part of your wonderful work and accomplishments as Light workers has been to join forces with the higher realms which has enabled us to work through and with your energies, and with your agreement, using your

will to direct these energies. Do you see, we did not take away your free will? Thousands of you have petitioned, "Thy Will Be Done," which allowed us to direct God's pure energy onto your earth as never before. Have we not told you that you are beacons of Light, anchors and conduits of cosmic energy?

And so, as the energy is increased and you absorb more and more of its transforming, revitalizing rays, you are feeling more and more of its effects. You are wondering when will you see the results; you have been feeling them, but when will the physical manifestation transpire? Soon, dear ones, much sooner that you can imagine. So, do not be concerned with a little dizziness and discomfort. This will soon pass, and you will be awed by what takes its place—new awareness, new vision, new spiritual gifts, new knowledge, yes, eventually, even a new body.

You will not be required to experience anything more difficult than you have already experienced. You have completed or accomplished the most difficult parts of your transformation. The rest of the way "is a breeze," as you would say. Enjoy your transformation, enjoy the return to your real identity, the real you. You will be greatly pleased at the completion of this particular phase of your evolution. And then on to higher and better things. We look forward to welcoming you to our world, dear ones; you are loved and missed. Love and blessings to you from Archangel Michael and the Masters.

5. Perfecting Your Telepathic Skills

Question: Dear messenger, please tell us how we may become better channels or perfect our telepathic skills so that we can bring forth vital information from the higher realms in its truest form.

Your question is one of great import at this time for it is imperative that as many of you as possible bring back into your awareness the long-lost faculty of telepathic communication, not only with each other, but with the higher realms. It is vital so that each of you will have the ability to receive direct information when needed. There will be coming events of a critical import in which time will be of the essence and, therefore, the only way information and instruction can be distributed is through direct contact with each individual soul, or person. It will not be possible to tell one channel and expect the information to be directed to all in their circle or those involved. It does not matter whether it is received through intuition or direct telepathic communication, but each person must tune into his own inner voice or transmission station.

Now, as to how this is best accomplished: First, there must be the desire—a strong and dedicated desire—which gives us permission to work with each person individually. When we say us, we mean guides, teachers, space brothers, angels, the Hierarchy, etc. Second, there must be a clearing process, a discipline of the mind. In other words, the ability to sit quietly and wait in the silence for the gentle nudgings of communication to begin—to be a receiver. Each person must dedicate himself to the highest truth and to the unselfish dissemination of information. The ego must be brought into balance, or tamed, so that people will realize that the

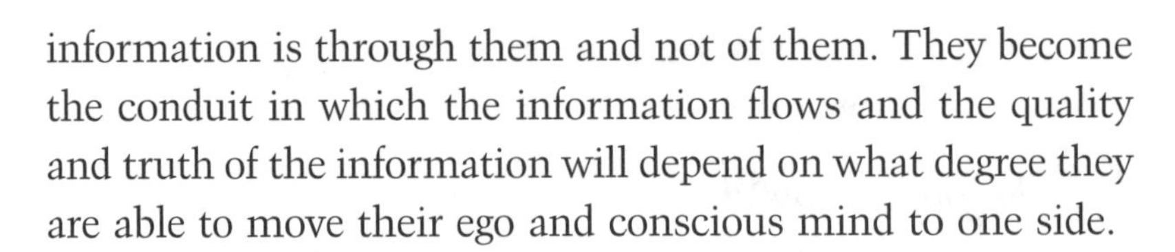

information is through them and not of them. They become the conduit in which the information flows and the quality and truth of the information will depend on what degree they are able to move their ego and conscious mind to one side.

So, there must be a purity of heart and purpose, dedication of will to accomplish or develop (or redevelop this ability), and then the faith to trust your abilities, or trust the information you start to receive.

As an exercise we would suggest: Sit quietly; surround yourselves with a protective light. Pay homage to the God Force or Father/Mother/God. Ask your Higher Self and I AM Presence for the teacher or messenger most compatible with your energies to come forth to work with you. In the unseen realms there are those who have their specialties, just as on your earth. You cannot expect to bring forth mathematical equations when you do not even understand algebra, or medical terminology, or detailed musical information, etc. if you do not already have this vocabulary or this talent within your memory bank. It is just too difficult for the teacher to convey this information through you. There are those who already are knowledgeable in these aspects or areas of endeavor, and it is best left to those who have these abilities. Then you can read or seek out what they have channeled. What each of you wants and needs to develop is the ability to convey or receive information pertinent to yourselves and to those in your immediate circle. Everyone is not destined to be a channel or cosmic telepathic receiver of great information to be disseminated to the masses.

The next step would be to develop the ability to place your consciousness in your crown chakra and then eight or ten inches above. Lift your spirit, so to speak; feel your

consciousness rise to meet the Masters. Leave your bodily awareness behind, and reach up into the ethers. We will feel your energy and we will begin to work with you. It will feel as if you are reaching upward, but it is really a turning inward process. It may be gentle nudgings at first, but they will get stronger, if you persist. Also, have specific questions in mind in the beginning. After a time, it will be possible to receive information of a general nature, but be specific in the beginning. Even questions where a "yes" or "no" answer can be given are advisable, and then wait for the impulse to come into your awareness. We are waiting for you—as many of you as possible—we can take care of all of you, or speak to you all at one time; we are not limited, dear ones.

Also, be prepared for the cleansing process to accelerate when you ask to become a channel of Spirit and, hopefully, you will also be prepared to take the advice given you. We are not available for parlor games or idle curiosity. It is best you not even try to contact the higher realms if this is your desire because all you will receive are pranksters or dissatisfied entities in the astral plane who will only misguide you.

The veils between dimensions are thinning and the energies are such that this wonderful gift is available to more and more of you, but you must step to the fore and say, "Yes, I am ready." In the beginning, it would be advantageous to set aside a certain time to practice these skills. This helps to discipline your mind and also lets the Masters know that you are serious in your seeking. We will move heaven and earth to bring you to your perfection, dear ones. Become Light-hearted and Light-spirited in your seeking, know that we are even more real than you and we are waiting to open the universe of all possibilities to you. Join us in bringing back the "real world" dear ones, a world of joy, a world of

love, beauty and peace, a world where we can interact freely and joyfully with you, and where you will have your validation as to our existence.

We await your endeavors; we await your questions. We await more joyous interactions with all of you. Come...come with us... hear the music and the singing of the spheres; come with us and flow in the ebb tide of Cosmic-consciousness where the Universal God Mind resides and where all things will be known to you. We have patiently awaited your awakening...it is time...COME.

Know that you are loved and cherished by Archangel Michael and the Masters.

6. Moving Through the Clearing Process with Ease and Grace

It is imperative that you all understand that you must go through a clearing process and some of you will find this is not always comfortable. However, this can be either relatively easy or very difficult. It is entirely up to you. You will know that something is amiss when physical problems begin to appear and also when you begin to have relationship problems or financial difficulties. These are representative of areas that need to be brought into balance, just as you need to balance your physical being with the emotional body, mental body and Spirit Self. Residual or unresolved issues are spewing forth so that, once and for all, you can bring them to resolution. This is your Soul Self helping you to confront these issues. It may not seem as if you are being helped, but this is the case, indeed. All unresolved issues, and these may be few or many, depending on how much inner work you have already done, must be brought to the fore and balanced so you can get on with your spiritual growth.

Remember, you have been told that it is necessary for fifty-one percent of your karma to be completed or resolved for you to be released from the Wheel Of Karma. At that time, you have cleared much of the illusion; you are well on the Path, and you are beginning to function as a Master. This is when the joy begins, when the way becomes smooth, blissful and exciting as you traverse higher and higher into the realms of all possibilities. This gift must be earned, dear ones. There are requirements and conditions, and all these must be met. But how will I know, you say? You will know when those you draw into your experience reflect the beauty of your soul; you will see yourself in their eyes. You will know when

you ask a question and the answer appears as if by magic. It sometimes just pops into your mind; or out of the blue, someone gives you the answer; or you find it in a book, or even from a movie or television. You will know when your abundance begins to flow as you accept and enjoy the bounty and let it overflow out into the world where it is most needed. You will know when your heart and soul sings and you cannot keep quiet; you must share your joy with anyone who is willing to listen. It is not to be held tightly under wraps; it is to be shared. This is one of the conditions. You will know when you begin to live in constant awareness of your spiritual heritage and feel the loving, living energies that you cannot yet see. All this is promised you, dear ones. Is the discomfort not worth it?

Accept each new challenge with eagerness. What is this person trying to teach me? What mirror is he reflecting back to me? What misconception am I holding that I need to experience this? What is my body trying to teach me? Listen, is it out of alignment? Are you giving it the attention it needs, via healthy food, exercise or movement, feeding it proper healthy ideas? Ideas and thoughts are food too, you know.

Time is of the essence, dear ones, you are needed, NOW. But first you must get your own house in order and your body in balance. You have all the help and resources you need, but you must ask and believe, then accept and acknowledge. Then you must take action. You must share what you have already experienced and learned and not stagnate—pass it on—make room for new and higher learning. You are not here to learn just for learning's sake. For your soul's sake, become an active participant in the evolution that is now taking place. Do not be left behind.

Never in the time of this cosmic day, and by this we mean during the evolution of humankind from its current inception, has there been such a golden opportunity for spiritual awakening, spiritual growth and transformation. The energies, wisdom, love, and transformational Light are awaiting you. You have available to you as much or as little as you wish, but you have the responsibility to clear your earthly vehicles and make way so that these dynamic new forces can create the miracle that you were truly meant to be. We leave you now. You are loved by Archangel Michael and the Masters.

7. Your Budding Consciousness of Light

What we wish to transmit to you today is how your awareness and attention to the details of your mind, the functional processes between your spiritual nature and your physical nature, create your reality and either further or deter your progress along the path of higher awareness or ascension.

When you were firmly entrenched in the third-dimensional reality, you were at the mercy of, or susceptible to, all of the currents or flow of energies of mass thinking or the emotions surrounding you on the astral planes which, as you know, interpenetrate and interact with the physical plane. As you begin to clarify your energies, releasing old conditioning, old half-truths and fallacies, you begin to expand your awareness to a finer attunement. This means, as a budding consciousness of Light, newer, purer truths begin to filter into your awareness.

Now, what many of you do not realize is that you have many of these higher truths buried in your spiritual consciousness, or soul's memory, waiting to emerge, but first the way must be cleared for this emergence. After you catch up, so to speak, with your stored level of awareness and incorporate it into your mental awareness, you are ready for the next level of instruction or spiritual attunement. Your soul or spiritual essence, or your Higher Self never loses the insight gained in its past experience. This does not mean that everyone brings this level of awareness down to the physical plane to be incorporated in his physical being, or physical way of being.

As you perfect and balance your physical, emotional, mental and spiritual bodies, there comes a time when these

combined energies reach a critical mass and there is an automatic incorporation or absorption of your soul's energies with those of your Higher Being or Oversoul's energies. At this point, there is a total interaction and harmony between these two levels of being, and the way is then open for the next level of awareness to be integrated. You are then, as a part of your Higher-consciousness, ready to receive direct instruction from your Christ-consciousness. This is a never ending process on the path to ascension back to the Creator.

This is ascension, dear ones. There are far more souls who take this path, one level at a time, than there are those who transcend in a flash of blinding light as the Christ Jesus did. This is the time of group ascension. Those of you who are in the vanguard, clearing the way, so to speak, agreed to help your brothers and sisters by your example. You have travelled this path many times in preparation for this particular event. Now the culmination and conclusion of this portion of your lifestream is at hand. Not the lifestream itself, but at this level.

All must evolve; nothing can remain static. There is a division as to who will move forward, or upward if you choose, and those who must retreat to other third-dimensional realities to continue their progress along the path of awareness. Those who are not quite ready for the next step in evolution will be the ones who will lead the next round of ascension, you see. You have also been in that position, so there is justice and perfection in the plan. They will not be forgotten; they will not be left alone; it is just not their time for graduation.

There are always those few who step out of the

mainstream and leap ahead of the masses. These are those brave, exceptional souls who dare to dream and be different and who have a vision within that they have not let themselves forget.

And so, specifically, what does this mean to you and those close around you? It means that the structures of society as you know it will be changing; loyalties will shift and it will seem the old ways of being and functioning will no longer be viable. Marriage, as you now know it, will not be the major focus of those on the higher spiritual path. There will not be a focus on one person but on the many. You will not have the luxury, if you wish to call it that, of devoting your time and energies to one person. You will be interacting with many, drawing energies and awareness from a larger family, a unity of spiritual awareness which you will need in order to function on the highest level required of you to accomplish the tasks and duties of the future. Your strength and dedication of purpose will be of utmost importance. You have been told you must bring all your physical connections into the proper perspective. You will not be required to give up all you know and love, although it is imperative that your attention be turned to the duties for which you have been groomed and commissioned to perform.

Stay Soul-centered, dear ones; keep your conscious attunement with your Higher Being, for the messages and instructions will be coming to you at a faster and faster rate. The time for waiting and preparation is over. The time of action is being initiated. There are different levels of awareness, as you can imagine; therefore, our messages will not be heeded or understood by all at this time. We will be transmitting messages of different vibrations and levels, and each of you will know if a message is meant for you for it will resonate

deep within your being. Take from each message that which you feel is right for you, but do not be discouraged or feel guilty if you are not ready to accept the full mantle of your spirituality. There are those who are ready to step forward and those who are not, just as in the initiation process. There has always been a secrecy in the different levels of the Brotherhood, or the higher levels of initiation. The inclusion of this knowledge must be earned and is not given idly. The process is being speeded up so that as many as possible can be reached and instructed. This is why you and those like you are so important. You not only conduct and anchor the Light, but you transmit the information that is being given to you so that others may come into their spiritual awareness, and they can see by your living example that it does work.

Accept your cloak of responsibility, dear ones. This is what you have studied, prayed, meditated and yearned for—your efforts have not been in vain. The fulfillment of your life's destiny is close at hand. Rejoice, rejoice, rejoice! You are ever guided and protected by Archangel Michael and the Masters.

8. The Urgency of Unity

What we wish to impart to you today is a new awareness. It is of the greatest importance that you begin to be an observer of your thoughts and actions and interactions every moment of the day and, yes, even of your nighttime activities, your dream state and twilight time. Awaken your senses, dear ones; be alive and a participant in creating the wholeness of the new you and your new surroundings. Become aware of the subtle energies at work, the little miracles all around and within you. We would like you to observe and recall the past month in which many of you have been going in different directions and experiencing various events, some wonderful and some disturbing. Think back and see or realize how much you have changed and how much has transpired in such a short span of time. Possibly, some of you may not see these changes within yourselves, but believe us when we say, there have been monumental changes within and without.

Your time frame or event structure is moving so quickly it is almost impossible for you to keep up and this may make you feel unsettled or somewhat out of sync. What we want to impress on you is that your earth is now in the whirlwind of change; the spiral of evolution is moving at an astonishing pace, and mostly for the good of all.

And so, what does this mean to you? And you all are saying, either consciously or unconsciously, "What do we do now?" We wish to inform you that the fourth and fifth dimensions are starting to crystallize on your dear planet earth. Areas of demarcation are starting to appear: Light here, darkness still there, suppression here, full awareness beginning to manifest there, etc. The turmoil that is being experienced is necessary to bring freshness and Light where it is most needed and, yes, to get the attention of those who are still so firmly entrenched in third-dimensional reality.

Each of you is being directed to where you should be for the present, yes, possibly in zones where devastation is predicted, or high crime, or stressful, depressed areas. But can't you see the purpose of this? You are needed for balance; you are needed as anchors; you are placed strategically where you will be of the most value and can be of the highest use in the master plan. And, let us assure you, dear ones, YOU ARE SAFE! You are not without protection...each and every moment. As long as you stay in tune with your inner self, you will always, repeat always, be apprised of what you should do or where you should be, unless you begin to buy into the reality of deprivation, destruction and cataclysm. Do you need this in your life or as a lesson? We think not.

Again, and time is even more critical, we encourage you to form your groups: three, four, nine, twelve, as small or as large as you wish, but meet, and meet often. Study, decree, meditate, pray together. Support, reinforce, inform each other. Help each other to realize that each moment of each day is critical...guard your thoughts and actions...you are powerful, dear ones. You have asked for enlightenment and many of you have evolved beyond the greatest expectations, but realize that as Masters-becoming, you are also co-creators with the Heavenly Host and the Ascended Masters. You are directed to create love, balance, peace and harmony in your personal universe—your body, Spirit, mind; your home, family, neighborhood; and then your city, state and on earth. All is beginning to vibrate at a higher rate and the only way to absorb and handle this energy without devastating results is through conscious awareness and concerted effort.

Many of you have felt the urge to relocate for various reasons and this may be proper, especially if the way is made clear and everything falls into place with ease. But this should not be done in panic and from fear. Remember, you must take yourself and your consciousness with you and if there is a deep-seated fear of destruction and cataclysm, you will draw this experience to you and it will come about no matter how far you run. You cannot hide from your Soul Self. We know that some of you are distressed and sad because you feel you are being separated from your spiritual family or your group is going in different directions. There is purpose in this, dear ones, and now that you are being reunited with your true spiritual family after so many aeons, you will not lose touch again. You may be separated geographically for a time, but you will be reunited and, remember, in Spirit you can not be separated. The time is soon coming when you will consciously have the ability to communicate across the miles telepathically...you now do this unconsciously, you see. Many spiritual gifts are soon to be yours as you complete your purification process and gain the wisdom and insight to handle these abilities with wisdom and discernment.

As your year begins its final phase, events will begin to happen even more quickly; there will be more unrest, more despair, more misery. Do not be caught up in third-dimensional activity or mentality. Feel compassion and spread your Light around the world, but do not become enmeshed in the turmoil. Part of your purpose at this time is to focus Light and energy on the coming elections and your government. Ask, petition, visualize coming to power the most worthy and highest-evolved souls available for the office, whoever these may be. Ask for enlightenment and follow your convictions; you will not be led astray.

You are now entering a critical phase as a species and as a planet in the evolutionary process on your way back to unity with the rest of God's creation. There is no doubt you will proceed to the next rung or spiral, just as the rest of your solar system, galaxy, and universe are doing. But will this be accomplished with grace and ease, with just minor adjustments and rearrangements, or will it need be by cataclysm and destruction? This is the urgency and why each of you is so important.

You are to be commended, dear ones, all of you who have worked so diligently and faithfully. You have made a difference and are assured your place in the new order, but it is not yet known if your sweet earth can make the giant step needed without the tribulation that has been so long predicted. This is why we speak to you with urgency...not to make you fearful or anxious, but to instill the immediacy of the situation. Do you not realize your power, and the power of unity, the power of dedicated focus and purpose? This is your mission at this time, dear ones. Meditate daily and nightly; better yet, become a living meditation so that every waking moment is focused on the highest purpose for all. Then bring your love and power together and create the meridians of Light and energy between you so that your strength is flowing back and forth amongst you and radiating out from you, both into the heavens and down to the center of your mother earth. Picture this flow of energy in your mind and see it growing, building, connecting, reinforcing, spreading through and around, building a framework of Light and love that will stabilize and cradle your earth and its inhabitants in such a glowing vibration of Christ energy that it will flow gently and with grace into the next dimension. This is your purpose, dear ones.

As you increase your dedication and use more of your abilities and energies, these will be increased ten-fold and then, again, ten-fold. You are all under the guidance of the Ascended Masters and the personal focus of countless angels. Can you not feel the difference in your life and in your awareness? No longer do you have to strive or walk alone. That time is past. It is now the time of unity—unity among humankind, and unity between humankind and Spiritkind. You no longer have to be isolated from us or we from you, and we rejoice at the reunion. We have waited long for the veil to be lifted, for your awareness to reach the point where we could, once again, communicate and interact with you. The process for many of you is nearing completion. Some of you are ready for the leap into the unknown, into the land of giants. And once you have taken the step, many of you will choose to help your brothers and sisters come into their awareness and, together, you will create the new order, the new Starkind of humanity who will create peace and harmony on your sweet planet earth. You will bring into your awareness how vast you really are, and will remember many of the talents and truths you have hidden within your soul-self. You will remember that you are already masters, that you have just forgotten...but now it is time to remember, dear ones. It is time for you to assume your true identity. Ask and you will be told; ask and it will come into your awareness; ask and the next step with be shown to you; ask, trust, and all will be given you.

Within each of you is all the power and wisdom you will ever need, for you have opened the direct lines of communication with the Masters. Direction may come in different modes, but it is there, beloved ones. Each of you who receives and takes to heart these messages is assured this:

YOU ARE IN DIRECT COMMUNICATION WITH YOUR HIGHER SELF AND THE MASTERS. Listen, feel, absorb and then transmit...you are a beacon of Light and energy and you are critical to the success of your earth and humanity's evolution. You are loved and protected by Archangel Michael and the Masters.

9. A Gift of Golden-White Energy Infusion from the Creator

Beloved Masters of Light, I bring you greetings from the Most High. Know how greatly you are loved and revered and how pleased we are with your progress in this great divine event called ascension. Let us smooth and erase some of your fears and frustrations, and assure you that you are achieving your goals, even though it may not be outwardly apparent to you.

We are aware of the vast amount of pressure many of you seeking the Light are experiencing, how harried and busy you have been, and of your deep desire to concentrate on your spiritual growth. As with the way of your world, there are tasks that must be accomplished and things you must attend to until completion. It is one of the trials and tests of the initiation process: your dedication and discernment, your ability to discipline yourself to attend to your worldly tasks and duties with willingness and joy. It is not yet time for you to release the things of the physical realm, no matter how much you might wish it; you must still take care of the details and mundane chores in your life.

You have the feeling that many things you are doing or experiencing will not happen again, or are coming to a completion, and this is correct. It is as if you are wrapping up, or summing up certain areas of your life's experience. Many of you do not realize that once you have firmly planted a Christed seed-thought in your consciousness or learned a lesson, you have transcended that level of experience. This is why so many of the events in your life you must go through alone. We can only help you once you make the commitment to operate from the focus of your higher spiritual awareness

and then we can smooth the way, but you must grasp the meaning and truth of an experience on your own.

Once you reach the level of being able to access your Higher Self, when you have brought your ego and personality under the guidance of your soul, instead of the other way around, we can begin to infuse you with greater Light, which brings wisdom and harmony, as well as protection from the mass consciousness. You then begin to incorporate more of your Soul-consciousness within yourself, building a wonderful new energy center which is anchoring above your heart and below your throat—the thymus area. You begin to function from a Soul-awareness reality, not the personality or ego awareness. This allows you to expand into a higher fourth-dimensional awareness (there are seven planes and many sub-planes in each dimension, you know), so that you can integrate and balance your emotional and mental bodies in preparation for the eventual emergence into a fifth-dimensional frequency where you will begin to connect with your Christ-consciousness and the en-lighten-ing of your physical being in preparation for ascension. The earth has now anchored the higher frequencies of the fourth dimension in preparation for its rebirth and it is a great gift to be able to step into that new awareness, a new universal consciousness. It is here and now, not sometime in the future. The earth is moving quickly through its evolution and refinement and if you wish to be a part of this most blessed transformation, you must raise your vibratory rate as well so that you will be in harmony with the earth and evolving humanity.

Dear ones, and we speak to all of you who are striving for your perfection, no matter what the level, the most important thing for you to do at this time is to focus on each day, each moment, creating love and harmony within yourself

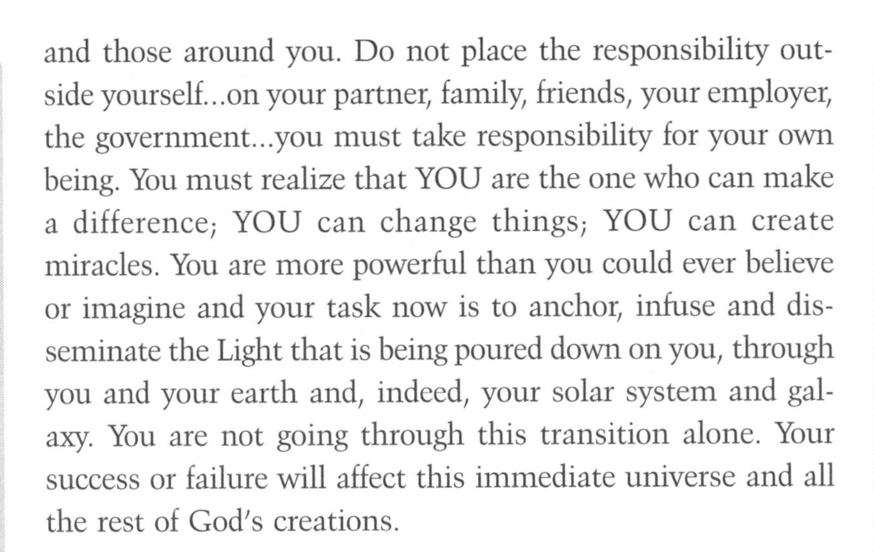

and those around you. Do not place the responsibility outside yourself...on your partner, family, friends, your employer, the government...you must take responsibility for your own being. You must realize that YOU are the one who can make a difference; YOU can change things; YOU can create miracles. You are more powerful than you could ever believe or imagine and your task now is to anchor, infuse and disseminate the Light that is being poured down on you, through you and your earth and, indeed, your solar system and galaxy. You are not going through this transition alone. Your success or failure will affect this immediate universe and all the rest of God's creations.

We sense your uncertainty, your desperation. We know you are asking deep within...can this all be true? Is it possible that we really do have help from the unseen realms and that, truly, there is a great change in the offing? Do you think you have been commissioned, nurtured and led for all these many aeons for us to desert you now? Why do you think we are making every effort, using every resource available to help you feel our presence and to relay our messages of hope and encouragement? You are a part of a vast army of Light warriors and you each have a specific duty to perform and a destiny to fulfill. You are coming to a culmination of all your vast learning experiences and are ready to assume your proper role in the monumental plan devised and decreed by Father/Mother/God and the mighty Forces of Light so long ago.

At this time, we wish to give you an exercise which will be most beneficial, that will help you to draw to you increasing amounts of pure divine energy from the Creator, thereby helping to anchor and to clear the pathway directly to your Higher Being and the I AM Presence that is dedicated to your spiritual growth and reunification.

Center your consciousness about one foot above your head and feel the pulsations of Christ energy begin to build and surge around you until it completely enfolds you. Envision it as a sparkling, golden white Light as you feel this energy begin to gradually flow down through your crown center, or chakra. Hold it there for a moment and feel its power increase until it permeates your head, the pineal gland, the pituitary gland, all of your brain cells and your third-eye chakra. Allow it to build and swell until you feel a fullness or completion and then let it flow into your throat area. Allow it to bathe the glands and muscles of your throat, energizing and activating this area so that as you learn and live the wisdom of Light and love, you will also be able to convey it clearly and truly with discernment. Now allow the energy to permeate your heart center, healing, clearing, washing away old residual pain and anguish, leaving a pure, pulsating vastness of Christ love energy. Feel the fullness in your chest area and be aware that you are building your spiritual armor in which no negative energy can ever penetrate if you hold fast to this perfect infusion of God's Love.

Feel the energy cleansing and purifying your emotional center, the solar plexus, balancing and releasing any impacted memories of aloneness, hurt and suffering. Remember, it is the emotional center that is of primary importance at this time, for it is the emotional body that must be brought into complete balance and under control if you are going to be given the gifts of mastership. A master is at all times in complete control of all the energy centers and no disruptive vacillation is permitted. We understand that this is a most difficult area for you to conquer, but as long as you begin to make a concerted effort, we will direct and help you in every way possible so that this can be

accomplished with the greatest ease and the least amount of stress.

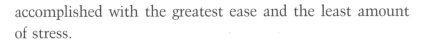

Now, let this precious energy drift down through the rest of your body and being, energizing and purifying, and allow the excess to flow from your fingertips and feet down into the earth...a gift of loving infusion from you to your dear planet to assist her in the release of stress and pain as she goes through her transition.

It may seem to you that we should focus on the remaining chakras also and not stop at the solar plexus, but we say to you, as you read this, if you feel a connection to our energy and feel the validation of truth in our message, then you have surely shifted your consciousness to the soul level of your being, away from the ego and the purely physical. Your body and all its parts will benefit and be balanced from the infusion of energy to the higher, transmuting centers of your being. And even though you must exist and function in the material world, you are focusing on your Light body, not your physical body. Your physical being can only follow in your path to perfection.

If possible, take time to do this exercise morning and night. It need not take but a few minutes and will be of momentous benefit. It will open the pathways for us to be in direct contact with you and to advise and guard you at all times. You see, your devotion and loving emanations enhance and empower us also, even as they do your brothers and sisters in the physical.

We will close now, but we do not leave you unattended. You are surrounded and protected and, as always, you are dearly loved by the Spiritual Hierarchy and the Masters of Light. I, Archangel Michael, bring you these truths.

10. Surround Yourself in Your Spiritual Armor

Your awareness and perception of what is going on around you and also in other realms and dimensions is increasing daily. You are truly beginning to function on a multidimensional level. What this allows is an integration of thought-forms and input from the higher realms. When you have the ability to access direct information you no longer have to rely on external sources and therefore you are functioning from Spirit.

Although you do not always awaken from your sleep time with full awareness, have no doubt that you are very active in your dream state. You are being taught, you are being trained in various ways, and the transmutation of your interior body is being speeded up and facilitated. Much of the initiation process is done during your sleep hours when your spiritual body is free of your physical body's restraint. Soon will come the time when you will be aware of these processes, but for now let us assure you that this is taking place.

You are beginning to feel the results of the transformation process which is working from the deepest level of your being outward. First you became aware of the expansion in your heart/soul area or heart chakra, the fullness and the delight of total, loving acceptance. Awareness is the first step and then integration follows close behind. You began to notice how you felt when you stayed focused in your heart center and open to the guidance of your higher consciousness, or your Higher Self. You also noticed the difference when you slipped out of this unity and back into third-dimensional thinking. It felt uncomfortable and heavy and you wanted that joyous, light, lovely feeling back. This has set the tone for your learning processes over the past year or so. Then gradually, you began to feel the lightness creeping into other parts of your body until now you feel as though you are filled with Light. You feel so full of this wonderful substance that at times it almost seems as if it is pushing against your body and expanding it. You have a feeling of hollowness, as if the real you is being restricted by the boundaries of your physical being. This is a different feeling and concept for you and not always comfortable.

You look into your mirror and you do not see much difference and you wonder why when you feel so much different inwardly. Is this not true? Do not let outward appearances fool you, dear ones. There are several processes in progress at this time within your physical being and spiritual being. First of all, your spiritual body, etheric body and awareness have made such a giant leap forward that it will take time for the rest of your lower bodies to catch up. Secondly, you are still working to release old, impacted, outdated energy stored in your cells and organs, and also you are still releasing old conditioning which is stored in your memory cells from ages past. Stepping out of third-dimensional mass-consciousness thinking and energy patterns is a very brave and difficult thing to do. You are not only battling (in a sense) your own thought patterns and conditioning, but that of the mass consciousness which fills the lower astral planes and surrounds your earth. This is one reason it is so important to surround yourself with protective, loving Light and energy. It is not that the "boogie man" will get you or some really negative, destructive energy will affect you in some way; no, you have evolved past that and are no longer subject to those lower energies. But you are susceptible to the emotional energy patterns, thought processes and popular concepts of the masses which swirl in a maelstrom in the ethers around you.

So you need to be aware and surround yourself with your spiritual armor, especially during these times when so many things are happening in your world. It will seem that it gets worse and worse, and it will until there is a shift in consciousness in enough people, and then it will begin to get better. You who are protected by the Light and who have risen above third-dimensional negativity will feel as though you are in the beautiful eye of the storm, in the calm serenity of a safe haven...and it will be so. Staying detached and keeping your emotional nature in balance is so important. By this we do not mean you are not to feel or express love or acknowledge your emotional nature; it is an important part of your being. But those around you may think you are callous or unfeeling when you do not express great distress or worry over situations that come into focus or happen around you. This is not the case; you are to assume the lofty outlook of the Masters: calmly, gently, lovingly standing by, observing, helping when possible, but allowing, not judging, for you know that all that is happening is for a reason and has purpose. Spread your loving Light and presence as far and wide as possible, dear ones. Counsel those who are led to you. By your actions you will be known, and those who have need of your Light and wisdom will be drawn to you.

Do not be concerned about the clearing of old energy patterns or karmic issues. If you do not fear the necessary changes, and give your Higher Self permission to oversee the process, time and the transmuting Violet Flame will work its magic in your behalf.

Many of you have anxiously awaited the call to service. You have asked and prayed that your mission would be made

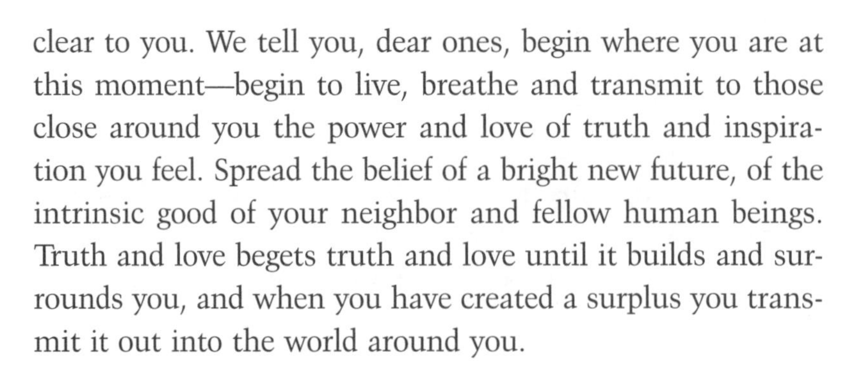

clear to you. We tell you, dear ones, begin where you are at this moment—begin to live, breathe and transmit to those close around you the power and love of truth and inspiration you feel. Spread the belief of a bright new future, of the intrinsic good of your neighbor and fellow human beings. Truth and love begets truth and love until it builds and surrounds you, and when you have created a surplus you transmit it out into the world around you.

Despair, hate and fear compound these energies and bind you in their grip. It always begins with you and spreads outward. Which world are you building for yourself and for your loved ones?

As you gain your spiritual strength, more and more will be opened to you: new awareness, new spiritual gifts, new relationships. You may lose old friends and acquaintances, but will be led to dynamic new groups and friendships—those with whom you have a destiny, a unity of purpose. Prayers are always answered, as you know, but in the best and proper time when you place yourself in the hands of Spirit. Just know that the most exciting time of your lives is fast approaching and you will not want to look back or return to your old way of being when it happens.

Live day by day, love moment by moment. Stay in your soul center and your heart center. Give those who need you your loving devotion and attend to the everyday mundane tasks for now. Your pleas to serve and desire to help humanity have not gone unheeded; we hear you and all those like you. The time to step forward and take up your spiritual banner is fast approaching.

You are fast approaching the time of momentous change. Changes that have been foretold for many aeons past and

have echoed down through the ages. It is as if your earth, solar system, the galaxy, and yea, the universe is at a pause, holding its breath, waiting for the explosion of cosmic energy to crescendo and carry all into that next higher realm, closer to that rarefied, pure domain of the God/Goddess/All That Is. It is ever drawing us closer, drawing us nearer and we stand in awe of our future together.

Ask and we will hear; call and we will join you in your endeavors; send out all the love that you hold and we will increase it a thousandfold. Your cause is our cause, for as you evolve, so evolves the universe. You are ever loved and protected by Archangel Michael and the Heavenly Host.

11. All Humanity Must Choose—Decision Time Is Now

What is the next step? Where do we go from here? Many of you are asking these questions and feel a discomfort and dis-ease as to your immediate future. What do the immediate future and the years beyond hold for you, those of you who are operating in the Light, functioning in the fourth dimension and reaching upward? We tell you this: there will be more and more physical manifestations and concrete experiences as to the validity of the messages and the new awareness that the higher realms have been bringing forth for you to incorporate into your reality. You will have validation as to our existence and you will begin to reap the rewards of your diligent application and supplication of loving decrees, mantras and prayers.

Many of the ancient lessons and rules of being and becoming are no longer valid. They are obsolete...you have evolved past them and their application. Therefore, new rules, new laws, new messages of wisdom are coming forth...messages that will stretch your imagination...force the boundaries of your thinking and your reality...new concepts, new formulas for everything from health, food sources, lifestyles, ways to accomplish higher levels of spirituality, to scientific application of electromagnetic energy and the earth's energy supply.

You have studied and learned about the seven Great Rays, the color spectrum of your physical plane, the seven energy centers in your bodies (or the seven chakras), and tried to incorporate this knowledge into your everyday living and consciousness. We tell you, dear ones, it is now time to take this learning further, into your future being. Instead of being under the influence of one major Ray or color and one

or more Subrays, it is now of the utmost importance that you begin to incorporate all the different Rays and their energies into your being. This must be done so that you can also begin to work with the five higher, more refined Rays that are being made available to you. You must no longer concentrate in just one area of endeavor, but must bring all facets of your nature into balance. As you begin to fuse and blend these energies, they activate the chakra centers in your body until they fuse into a blinding white, iridescent swirling light and activate the eighth, ninth and higher energy centers, thereby clearing the way for your perfected fifth-dimensional Light body and your awareness of your higher Christ-consciousness, your I AM Presence.

We speak now to those of you who have worked so diligently to create a loving, forgiving nature, to walk the path of nonjudgment and to stay in communion with your soul, or Higher Self. You will notice that strife and distressful events are becoming more removed and less frequent within your immediate circle of experience. You are affected less and less by outside events and other people. You carry in your heart center a vast amount of love and compassion, but you do not allow things that transpire outside yourself to have a negative effect on you and your more perfect realm of reality. You are in the process of building a fifth-dimensional reality and it begins within your innermost core and spreads outward. First it affects you and your body, then your home and your loved ones and then out into your neighborhood, city and then, on and on. And as your reality connects to that of your sisters and brothers in the Light, it takes on strength and becomes more powerful and builds faster. So you see what you are creating with your dedicated, purposeful actions of love and thought power?

There will be a brief lull of energy between now and the end of your current year. This will give you all time to assimilate the vast amounts of accelerated energy that have recently been directed to you and your planet. Take this time to perfect your skills, to incorporate your new knowledge and reinforce your new ways of acting and being, for after the lull, there will again be an acceleration and an impaction of energy focused on your planet. Make a decision now, in your consciousness and in your verbal interaction with others, that this new infusion will not bring more destruction, violence and negativity. You can focus and channel this energy into positive forms, modes and accomplishments and not allow it to run amok among the masses of the unenlightened. You, as Light warriors, are becoming more powerful and are able to assimilate more of the incoming energy and funnel it into positive action, rather than allow it to be drawn toward and used by those who operate via greed and self-destruction.

Focus your attention and send positive thoughts and loving reinforcement to your government. Let them know that no longer will you tolerate ineptitude and corruption, or self-serving legislators to run your country. Let them know that they will be held accountable and you will not stand by and allow them to spend your country into bankruptcy and oblivion.

The cosmic web of spiritual awareness is being drawn tighter and tighter. It is being energized and fine-tuned so that all those who are out of sync will become more dissatisfied, more uncomfortable, more frustrated. They will be forced to take a stand...they will no longer be allowed to "ride the fence," so to speak. They will be given every opportunity to accept the way of Light and truth, but the law of free will is still in operation and it must be their choice.

Therefore, the coming years will see a vast disparity in the lives of people: those who have chosen the way of Light and life will see wondrous miracles happening to them and around them, and those who choose to remain in the third-dimensional prison of darkness and negativity will see the bonds of this prison drawing tighter and more restrictive until they will cry out in anguish. Some will then choose to surrender and will be shown the way and led out of the darkness into the Light. But many will remain so enmeshed and trapped in their habits and old ways of thinking and being that they cannot break free. These are the poor souls who will experience the cataclysmic events and the destructive forces manifested by their own negative thought-forms. Send out your loving thoughts of peace, and the magic power of the Violet Transmuting Flame, but do not become involved in the negative energy or the fear patterns of the masses. Stay removed and distant in your emotions. Help in whatever way you are led, be it physical, mental or spiritual, but remain in your fourth- and fifth-dimensional reality. We admonish you, dear ones, this is of vast importance; you serve no purpose and do no good if you allow your emotions and mental bodies to once again become entrenched in the restrictions of negative energy.

Always remain the observer, always stay heart-centered and soul-focused, thereby drawing on your higher strength and the wisdom of the unseen realms around you. Guard your thoughts and your words, discipline your thought patterns and emotional nature and you will soon walk among the Masters. Your time of graduation is drawing nigh, my beloved ones. Your daily routines may seem to be the same, sometimes exciting, sometimes boring, but trust us when we say there is far more going on and being accomplished

that you can ever imagine. Gather together for loving interaction and reinforcement among your spiritkind and know that where you gather, we, too, are with you. You are ever loved and protected by Archangel Michael and the Masters.

12. Abundance: Personal and Planetary

Our message today is to help you to be more aware of your thought processes and to encourage you to release old, outmoded concepts. It is vastly important that you begin to think clearly and focus on the emotions and thought-forms you emit throughout the day and night, for as you begin to function in the higher fourth and the fifth dimensions, these will manifest very quickly. Are you creating beauty, peace and harmony, or are you contributing to the negativity that is running rampant throughout your world?

Specifically, let us speak of abundance. There is great concern today about jobs, money, or lack thereof, uncertainty about the future, and a helpless frustration as to how you are going to feed the world. How do you feel about abundance? Do you believe you deserve love, health, wealth and prosperity? Perhaps you think you do and you affirm day after day that wealth and prosperity are yours, and yet you look on those who have great wealth with disdain and mistrust. You judge them for not sharing and using their wealth for the good of all, or you think they are frivolous and unworthy. Know that you, too, have misused wealth and power in many, many lifetimes and know also that this is part of the learning process. Allow them their lessons and do not act as their judge and jury, thereby shutting the door to your own prosperity. It takes time and soul evolvement to learn that great wealth in itself will not bring happiness. Look around and see how miserable and discontented many of the very wealthy are. This should tell you something.

All the beauty and abundance, opulence and wealth of the universe are yours for the asking, but there are rules and responsibilities that go with these gifts, as with any other.

You must hold these gifts lightly in your hands and heart, and know that they are on loan to you and that you must let them flow through you and back out to be shared by all, and then even greater things will be given you. They are not yours to horde and hide; it is not appropriate to spend all your time and energy in maintaining or trying to hold on to your treasures. It is your misconception of riches, your emotional attachment, your misplaced importance of money and possessions that create problems and unhappiness.

You have read and been taught that you must release all to the Creator; you must be willing to relinquish all you hold dear in the world, and this is true. Only then, paradoxically, will all be given to you, for then you realize that riches are not what make you happy. It is not in wealth where your security and well-being lie, but in your spiritual awareness where all things are possible to you. Then you can enjoy the bounteous life and walk in wondrous beauty and grace as you manifest heaven on earth, the way the earth was meant to be and will soon be again.

You must ask yourself, "What do I truly believe about my abundance?" You must dig deeply into your subconscious and resolve any conflicting issues you may have from past or present lifetimes, so that your conscious and subconscious minds are in harmony with your Higher Self and willing to accept all that is good and perfect. Then you will allow abundance to flow freely into your life and out into the world.

Do not be afraid to desire and ask for great wealth and bounty so that you can show others how it should be used and distributed for the good of all—not to make others dependent or as a do-gooder with a holier-than-thou attitude, but to create opportunities, to inspire, to help establish a

more equitable distribution of wealth to those who are striving to better themselves and who are reaching for their higher purpose. What a wonderful gift to give or receive!

The wealth of your country and the world will, in the not too distant future, be redistributed. It will be taken away from those who have not earned it honestly and who operate from a standpoint and mentality of greed, excess, power and self-importance. Countries and individuals will see that their wealth is beginning to disappear, to slip through their hands and cease to flow. Miraculously, it will be placed into the hands of those who have evolved to a higher state of being and awareness so that it can be rechanneled for the use and benefit of all humanity, placed in the responsible hands of those who realize that all humankind is as one. When one person or one race is ill or suffering from deprivation, the whole suffers, just as your body does when you develop cancer or any other life-threatening illness. It remains isolated for a time but then rapidly spreads to the whole being, debilitating, weakening, until it encompasses and destroys the entire body.

Even the homeless in your country, especially in areas with beautiful, warm climates and surroundings, should be grateful and thankful that they are not homeless in Africa or Asia or many of the other lands around the world. They have much to be thankful for and if they would, day by day, gradually take responsibility for their abundance and create a feeling of thanksgiving and expectation, they would see miraculous things happen. What do they have to be thankful for, you might ask—for the mild climate, the sunshine, for compassionate people who give them encouragement and help where possible, for tolerance and, yes, a great deal of understanding, much more than in other countries around

the world. There are those dear souls who are dedicated to feeding and nurturing these people and who give unselfishly and lovingly of their time and energy. They are indeed to be commended and will be blessed for their efforts.

This brings us to another misconception. Many of you feel guilty or confused because you feel you are not doing enough for this effort or that cause. Let us clarify this for you. Each of you comes into this lifetime and every lifetime with a specific mission and a destiny to fulfill. Each of you, in many lifetimes, has been a server of humanity, a martyr to a cause, and has sacrificed your comfort and well-being for others. You, who are the vanguard of the New Age, the Light bearers, have a different mission, a mission of greater scope. You have not been directed to minister to those who have need for nurturing and food for the body, but to nurture those who seek food and sustenance for the soul. Each is of equal importance, for how can a being reach for spiritual perfection until he or she has food and comfort for his physical being? So never feel guilty that you are not physically involved with feeding and caring for the deprived. You, in concert with the higher realms, are focusing and channeling a new awareness, a new level of evolution where some day all will realize that there is no such thing as shortage, deprivation or lack in the higher states of being, and that this is your destiny.

As the vibrational level of the earth is raised and expanded and as the human body begins to resonate at a finer attunement, it will come into the mass consciousness that you are entitled to all the bounty and abundance you can imagine. You will not have to guard your riches or your borders or lock your doors, for it will be there for all to partake of and enjoy. Oh, the joy that will be realized when you truly cross

the boundaries of your consciousness and see all humanity as your brothers and sisters. The floodgates of all Creation's abundance will open and flow freely throughout your earth. Brotherhood, peace and abundance: this is the meaning of the New Age, dear ones. It will not happen tomorrow or next year, but it is beginning and it is mushrooming rapidly. Your government and others in the world are gaining a heart and a new awareness. They are beginning to tap into their heart center, and gradually assume the responsibility for their actions and for the welfare of the people. Power, control and self-serving attitudes will no longer be tolerated and can no longer be hidden.

It is not to your advantage that they do more for you, but it is their responsibility to act as leaders, compassionate directors and examples, and to allow each country, state, community and person the opportunity to become self-sufficient, self-aware and self-sustaining. You do not need more government intervention, but more government direction and example.

And so, dear ones, begin to fine-tune your emotions and your thought processes. Do not let the turmoil and the agony of world events color your perception of perfection. Stay focused in your affirmation of peace, abundance and harmony, for it begins with you and spreads outward. Every step, every accomplishment you make in your spiritual evolvement toward perfection is a contribution to the whole. Your saying, "Let there be peace and let it begin with me," is more profound and dynamic than you will ever know.

As you move through the momentous years ahead, do seriously take stock of what you have accomplished...how far you have come and what has transpired. Seriously consider

what it is you need to release and resolve within yourself and your immediate world. Do not let a new year begin with disharmony in any area, be it relationships, work, unresolved issues within yourself, whatever is keeping you from realizing your communion and interaction with your Higher Self and your Christ-consciousness. Wondrous gifts of awareness await you, dear ones. As you clear the pathway of communication and interaction with that greater part of your being, you begin to realize how limited you have become. It is time for you to assume your true identity. Promise yourself that you will reach out for the gift of wholeness, that your main focus from this time forward is to reunite with all the myriad parts of yourself so that you will, once again, be that perfect Light being that originally came to this earth so many aeons ago. Make this your mission. We are ever near to help you every step of the way. You are loved and cherished by Archangel Michael and the Masters.

13. The Clarion Call to Unite Is Sounded!

Beloved children of Light, we, the messengers and servants of the Creator, again sound the Clarion Call for all the mighty forces and Legions of Light to come forth and unite. You who have been scattered throughout the ages and throughout the universe are now gathered here on the blessed planet earth to assist in the birth of a new awareness, a new unity, a new reality. You have suffered the separation from your spiritual family, from your higher awareness, from your sense of unity with the God Mind. You have allowed yourself to be drawn into the web and restrictions of duality: duality in your brain function; the establishment of a shadow self which you believed was your enemy, and therefore you must deny it and do battle with it in order to conquer and overcome; the duality outside yourself of male and female energies, not realizing these were active and functioning within. Your struggle is about balancing these internal energies, not the external ones which validate your picture of reality.

You established riches and plenty and then lack and deprivation; you created schools of great knowledge, forgetting that wisdom comes from within. Knowledge without wisdom is hollow and leads only to a cluttering of the mind with facts and figures, but does not assist you to create a sense of balance and harmony. You came to look upon your physical being, your ego and your mind as the ruler of your universe, and put Spirit and God somewhere "out there" beyond yourself and out of reach. You began to believe in a system of good and bad, right and wrong, light and dark, strong and weak, holy and evil, superior and inferior, you and your concepts and ideas versus all others.

All of these things were created to enhance and build the

feeling of separation, aloneness, by those who could only gain strength by dividing and conquering. THAT TIME IS PAST, DEAR ONES!

It is time to reunite, to reestablish the strength and unity of the God Force of which you are an integral part.

First, you must reunite all the myriad parts of yourself in a harmonious, loving, vibrating vehicle of Light. Reestablish communion and the harmony of your brain structure, realizing it is a fully functioning perfect unit of wisdom and power. This will initiate and reconnect many of your latent abilities that have diminished over the ages from non-use. Realign and reunite the male and female energies within you, focusing love and Light on your shadow self. It has served you well and has valuable knowledge to impart if you will call a truce and join forces.

You must stop looking outside yourself for validation of self-worth, love, success and truth. You have within you all that is necessary for spiritual awareness, happiness, abundance and, yes, ascension. You have within you your own divine I AM Presence, and your own individualized Christ-consciousness. It is not "out there"; it is within you.

The divine wisdom and knowledge within you which was divided, blanked-out, restricted, and kept from your awareness all these many ages past is also being restructured, plugged in, reinforced and even added to in order that you will, once more, realize your divinity and from whence you came.

It was also necessary for you to be divided and separated from your twin flame and your spiritual family so that you would have to function on your own, under your own power, following your own experiences and lessons. You are an integral facet or part of your spiritual unit and of the Divine Whole, adding a uniqueness that only you can supply. Therefore, it was necessary for you to strike out alone—seemingly, only catching glimpses of your divine complement and spiritual family now and again, mostly in dreams, yet sometimes, when you were faltering or near defeat, in the physical, to give you courage and hope to continue the long, painful struggle.

We are here to tell you that those times are quickly coming to an end, dear ones. You are experiencing the gathering of your spiritual family, one by one...glorious recognition and the feeling of love and unity beyond compare, the feeling that, at last, you no longer have to struggle alone, the wealth of wisdom, knowledge and talents to share, the strength and courage to venture forth into the uncertain, uncharted territory, hand in hand, shoulder to shoulder, unified in loving purpose, supporting each other, encouraging, lifting, gaining new awareness and power through synergy and the dynamics of numbers.

Many twin flames are miraculously being reunited to complete their last lifetime in the physical on earth together. At last, coming together in their wholeness, they bring a divine complement to each other, not looking for a missing part, but an enhancement to the whole. Many of you who will choose to complete this life's experience without a mate, will instead find all your needs for love and emotional support being supplied by a myriad of people, male and female, in such a wonderful, rewarding way that you will not miss the one-on-one relationships you once felt were so important.

Dear ones, we are asking you to begin the process of inner

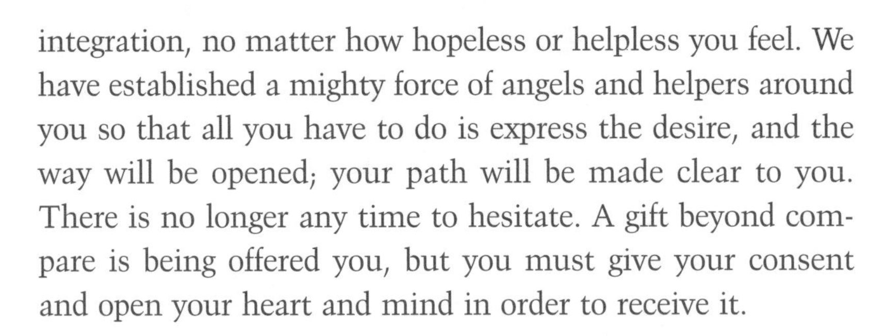

integration, no matter how hopeless or helpless you feel. We have established a mighty force of angels and helpers around you so that all you have to do is express the desire, and the way will be opened; your path will be made clear to you. There is no longer any time to hesitate. A gift beyond compare is being offered you, but you must give your consent and open your heart and mind in order to receive it.

Examine all the areas of your life that are out of balance, where there is disharmony and disunity. See yourself encased in a blazing light of divine awareness and ask to be shown the areas that are most in need of attention. Let go of old, outworn crusts of protection: vanity, self-doubt, fear, feelings of isolation and unworthiness. Promise yourself, here and now, that you will reach out from your heart's center, with love and longing, for the reunification of your whole being, the master you are, and then to the many magnificent beings that comprise your spiritual family. This is the giant step you are being asked to take.

This is the call we are putting forth: "UNITE, BELOVED ONES. IT IS TIME ONCE AGAIN TO GATHER OUR FORCES, TO MAKE READY FOR THE MIGHTY MARCH ACROSS THE HEAVENS, REESTABLISHING THE DOMINION AND POWER OF ALL THE LEGIONS OF LIGHT...THE FORCES OF GOD!"

The establishment of heaven on earth can only come to pass through the unified force of all our spiritual family. You and all those like you are vital to the effort. This is why you came to this place so long ago. This is why you were allowed to return at this particular time...many asked to come; only those who stayed true to their mission from the beginning were given permission.

Soon to come will be what you might call a "media blitz" and it will be worldwide. In ways you could never imagine, the new awareness will be brought to the masses. It is already building slowly, via movies, television, news articles, books and, most powerfully of all, by word of mouth. The time for isolation and secrecy of your mission as Light warriors is over. The masses are stirring and beginning to clamor for information, answers and solutions. Be ready, dear ones. Many of you have asked to know your mission; soon you will have no doubt.

We rejoice in anticipation; we revel in your success, brave and faithful warriors. Allow your hearts to swell with joy and love and know the time of reunion is at hand. I AM Archangel Michael.

14. The Path

The outward path we travel
Is fraught with sorrow and pain,
But we must experience all in order to attain
Wisdom and perfection on this earthly plane.
When at last we take the inward path
To that glowing, perfect place,
We start the long climb upward
Where, again, we'll see God's face.

Ronna Herman

15. Embrace Your Fears— Accept the Challenge

Beloved children of Light, I, Archangel Michael, come to you on this powerful and significant day, the day of the full moon and a total lunar eclipse as well. The moon represents the fullness of your nature: your intuitive, creative source; your shining empowered self. The eclipse represents your shadow self, the darkening or suppression of your Spirit...or your fear. Look at your fears, dear ones, for they are the very emotions you must embrace, that you must face. Your fears are what is keeping you from your dynamic empowerment—your masterhood. Your fears are what is holding many of you in bondage in the third dimension.

Once more, let us assure you, you have nothing to fear. Many of you are caught up in the "Age of Cataclysm." You fear it will happen, and you also fear it will not happen, because if it doesn't, how will you know that the New Age is really here and all you have been told is true? You want to believe all the stories of the wondrous times to come, but how can you be sure? Look around you; look within, and if you cannot see the vast difference that has been wrought in the last decade, maybe your world is not changing. Maybe you are so caught up in fear and denial that you will not allow yourself to accept and support the new awareness and vitality that is permeating your earth and much of humanity.

Become a friend and companion to your fears, face them head on and affirm that you are going to use this energy to create positive results, not stagnation. Do you fear becoming a master because of the responsibility it will bring? Do you hesitate to accept your creativity and to use your talents because you fear you will be judged and you think your efforts

will not be good enough? Do you fear if you become too "different" your family and friends will ridicule or reject you? Do you fear if you step out into the unknown world and trust your Spirit to support you in manifesting your abundance, you will become impoverished? Do you fear you may become successful and you are not sure you can handle the responsibility of that success? How will you know, how can you tell unless you accept the challenge and step out into the unknown, the uncharted territory?

We tell you this, either you move forward and accept the challenge or your Spirit will force you to face whatever issues are most important to your growth, and this may mean confronting your worst fears after they have manifested. As surely as you avoid that which is best for your growth, just as surely it will manifest in your reality. It is the time of awakening, dear ones; the time for hedging and delay are over. Why not use the vibrant gifts being offered you to move with grace and ease through all the remaining issues that need to be resolved?

Many of you are experiencing tests and trials in your daily lives, but are not caught up in the negativity. You see these situations for what they truly are—misqualified energy being brought into balance and perfection. You move through your days in the serene knowledge that all is as it should be, that "This, too, shall pass," and you are practicing the art of co-creation, of becoming a master. A master must serve an apprenticeship...it does not just happen. There are lessons, tests and experiments and then, finally, graduation.

And so we implore you, as Spiritual Warriors, use your fears for your growth, draw on the strength of your Christ Self and wield the sword of power and truth to cut through

the bonds of limitation. We see so many of you filled with knowledge and desire, bright with promise, but afraid to challenge the status quo, afraid to step out into the unknown.

The status quo and your world as you know it will change, with or without you, dear ones. If you could begin, day by day, to follow your Spirit with joy and without hesitation, to accept each challenge and opportunity with enthusiasm and the assurance of victory in the end, think of the burden that would be lifted. Think of the joy of living each day in anticipation of what is ahead, of the empowerment you would feel.

You have heard, time and again, to live in the moment, that today is all you have. We tell you that you have an eternity, but you must decide how you will experience eternity. A day lived in joyful purpose seems only a moment, and a day lived in fear and hesitation may seem an eternity.

Fear manifests in many forms: anger, denial, pain, illness, lethargy, depression and sadness. It is restrictive, crippling, damaging, and feeds upon itself when turned inward and allowed free reign. Never before have you had so much help, so many sources from which you may draw wisdom, encouragement and support. But you must take the first step; it is you who must turn and face yourself directly and affirm, "Today I will do that which I fear the most. I will take my fear in hand and with its power I will surmount any obstacle I envision."

You ask for validation as to the truth of New Age wisdom, and we say to you, it is up to you to supply your own proof. We can only supply the energy and loving support; it is up to you to manifest it in your world of reality. Look around you; see the miracles happening to others, day by day. They

are no different than you, except they have embraced the gifts and opportunities that have been offered to them. You have no way of knowing what trials and obstacles they have overcome on their way to masterhood, no way of knowing how much or how little they had to work with, or what seeming sacrifices they have made. You see only the end result. Be assured you have the same opportunities, the same strengths and resources if you will only claim your heritage.

You are unique; there is no other quite like you. You came empowered with unique strengths, and restricted with unique memories of limitation. You are a facet in the shining sphere of the God Mind and have a specific task to accomplish. The more difficult the task, the more strength and abilities you have imprinted within your memory and on your soul, so none has more or less, or is better than another; only in your uniqueness do you differ. The God Mind is desirous of experiencing every imaginable manifestation, with the ultimate goal of full awareness and perfection. Turn your gaze toward perfection, dear ones. See within yourself the glimmer of the jewel you are, unlock the door to the wisdom and power within you and you will create miracles untold.

Do not allow the fear and negativity that is spewing forth from your media, from your government and the mass consciousness to make an impact on your awareness, my precious ones. This is perhaps one of your greatest tests at this time, to stay serene and in loving assurance of who you are, where you are going, and what is being manifested in your world—all because of your bold, dynamic actions and beliefs. The refinement (or unrefinement) of the energy you emit from your thoughts is building your new reality just as surely as if you were building a home, brick by brick, day by day. Build a mansion, dear ones; build a glorious, shining, loving

world filled with all possibilities, surrounded, permeated and enriched with peace, harmony and joy.

We are ever near to assist you, to lend gentle guidance and encouragement, but you must reach up and boldly draw forth the empowerment and perfection of the higher dimensions and claim them as your own. I, Archangel Michael, the Legions of Light, and the Heavenly Host embrace you.

16. It Is Time to Resolve Your Relationship Issues

Your lessons of love, acceptance and tolerance will be coming to you more and more rapidly as the energy infusions are increased. This is so you will have an opportunity to resolve all residual issues that are keeping you from becoming your pure Christ-consciousness.

Relationship issues are of the greatest import at this time, resolving and clearing karmic imbalance and also coming to terms with any disharmony in your present relationships. Take a look around you or take an inventory of the people by whom you are influenced, and at those you influence—at home, at work, friends, relatives. What is your relationship with these souls: stressful, discordant, frustrating; or supportive, loving and fulfilling? The love, balance, and harmony you derive from a relationship is of vast importance, for this expands your Christ-consciousness and increases the Light and vibrations in your etheric field, and then in your physical body. Any discord or disharmony compresses and suppresses the energy of love and retards your growth, dear ones.

The emphasis is on relationships so you can learn to accept your spiritual brothers and sisters in all their imperfections, and love them for the Spark of the God Force within, no matter how dim or small. This is why we have stressed love and acceptance of self, for how can you become tolerant of others and accept their faults if you cannot accept and forgive yourself?

Evolving to and through the fourth dimension as a precursor to mastership in the fifth dimension means coming to an awareness that you are a part of the All That Is, an integral part, and therefore worthy of love. It is about turning

inward and seeking the power and truth that is lying dormant, waiting to be called forth. It is about clearing the channels that have been blocked for many aeons so that you are once again able to communicate with your home base, and your Spiritkind. You perhaps are not aware how significant the phrase "E.T., Phone Home" really is. We are waiting for you to reconnect, to clear the static and distortion of fear, hate, judgment and limitation so that you will be able to phone home, and we will answer. Many of you are doubtful, surprised, or in awe of those who have the ability to communicate with the unseen realms (and more of you are regaining this ability all the time), but know that this is the normal state of your being, dear ones; you have just forgotten. You have been disconnected for so long, you do not remember the time when this was a natural part of your sense structure.

The fourth dimension is about accepting your divinity, re-aligning yourself with the forces of the God/Goddess instead of the forces of third-dimensional limitation. The fourth dimension is where you will begin to work in unity with all the forces of nature, your precious mother earth and the emissaries of heaven to bring about the return of the Garden of Eden. The earth at its inception was the Garden of Eden, and to that state she will return, with you, or without you. Do you not want to be one of those who is assured a place in that glorified utopia?

As you begin to control your emotions and bring your four lower bodies into harmony and control, not only do you begin to operate in the realms of the higher fourth dimension, but you then have the capability of tapping into the lower realms of the fifth dimension. You begin to create and manifest your own existence, your own world as a co-creator with

the God Force. So you see why it is so important that you bring all facets of your being under control, into unity and love? You hear these words over and over, in various ways, but they are the most important words you will ever hear.

The electromagnetic energy is being showered on you and your world as a gift. It is up to you how you use this gift, or not use it. Your Soul Self has been waiting for aeons for this event. Are you going to let it pass you by because it takes a little work or effort on your part? Anything that comes into your consciousness at this time is for your growth and resolution; it is a gift. Your Higher Self is trying to gently nudge you along the right path, in the right direction. So, dear ones, look at your relationships; resolve any issues that are not allowing you complete loving harmony. If you cannot resolve a relationship issue on the physical level, turn inward. Seek your inner power—your Soul Self, in the temple of your heart—and bring forth into your mind the person in question. Speak to them at a soul level, just as you would in person. Ask their forgiveness (even if you feel you are not at fault), send love to their Soul Self, tell them you love them and feel the love flowing from your heart center to their heart center. Bless them and surround them with the golden white Light of the Christ-consciousness. This is more effective than you can ever imagine, as long as you do not return to the old pattern of discord. When a particular person comes to mind, see him filled with and surrounded in the Violet Transmuting Flame and ask for his "highest and best good."

You have worked long and hard to bring your mental and emotional nature into balance, to open your heart center. Now it is time to begin using this new empowering energy; it is time for action, for results. Reading, studying, theorizing will no longer suffice, dear ones. ACTION is the word

of the day, bringing all you have learned into reality, into fruition.

You who have asked and prayed to be of service are being alerted to make ready, to prepare to come forth, cloaked in your spiritual armor without, and with your spiritual awareness within, to spread the message, to be a living example of the new humanity: the fusion of Spiritkind with humankind. We have told you it is important for you to gather together with your spiritual brothers and sisters to anchor the Light, to reinforce and direct the energies being sent to your immediate locale. We now tell you that you must also begin to go forth and share your awareness with others...to encourage, to counteract the negativity and fear that is circulating, to tell people that there is hope, there is a way, there is help and, yes, the future is bright, if they will only accept it. Even a little at a time, even a small change in attitude and thoughtforms makes a vast difference.

Begin by changing your perception; welcome the opportunity to resolve any residual issues in your personal world, instead of seeing them as trials, tests and obstacles. See how quickly they disappear, never to return, once you have treated them with the MAGIC OF LOVE IN ACTION. Be aware of the many miracles taking place in your world every day. Know that you ARE creating; you are building your new world, from the inside, out.

When others moan and lament about the state of the world, point out the positive things that are happening. Focus on the wonders that are taking place, but gently, dear ones, gently. Do not make light of their pain or their problems, but encourage them to look at them in a different way, or just turn the conversation to another topic and do not buy

into the scenario. Do not add to the negative energy that is being spewed out into the ethers.

The focus is being narrowed in various areas—different tasks being assigned, if you will. The focus on the western coast of the United States is to stabilize and release the tension and stress buildup in your mother earth by neutralizing the negative energies of the mass consciousness—the gray, swirling mass of negativity that encompasses your land in the astral plane. Much energy was infused in southern California during the time of the awakening and many Light workers were drawn there because of this. Much growth and soul-awareness was realized, but also, much of this incoming energy was used in a negative way—bringing chaos, destruction and violence.

There is a great opportunity to return this precious land to its former pristine beauty, a golden opportunity to draw those who are suffering and headed in the wrong direction onto the path of Light. Do not abandon your homeland; it is worth saving. Dedicate yourself and your efforts to recapturing the dream of days past—the land of opportunity, the land of the future. Draw from deep within your soul's memory and recall the beautiful paradise of the land called Lemuria. Many of you who once walked those shores have returned to help rectify the past mistakes that resulted in the sinking of a vast land mass so that it could be cleansed and purified. That need not happen again, dear ones, if you will only heed the warnings and embark on a path of correction and recovery.

You, as empowered Light warriors, have the ability through your joint efforts—meditating, praying, and decreeing together—to neutralize a vast amount of this negative energy.

This is your assignment; this we commission and implore you to do, dear ones. We will join you in your efforts; we will infuse you with multitudes of Light and energy in unified purpose, which you will transmit down into your sweet earth and into the ethers of your cities. This is how you are being asked to begin your mission. Will you accept? Alone, you make a great impact; together, you have the force of Heaven behind you. Until we come together again, know you are protected and loved. I AM Archangel Michael.

17. A New Awareness of Life and Death

Beloved children of Light, let us delve into the mystery of death and the misconceptions that humanity has with the process. Humankind either looks upon death with dread, or tries to ignore it entirely, as if quite possibly they can either forestall this inevitability or fool themselves into believing they are immortal. The truth of the matter is that both of these beliefs are valid, but for quite different reasons.

One of the greatest benefits of the process you are now experiencing (and we acknowledge that it can be quite uncomfortable and painful) is that when you realize and complete your transmutation, you will no longer need to experience the death process, or the reincarnational process either. The process as you experience it now causes you to take on the veil of forgetfulness and seemingly start from scratch, or at the beginning, every time you enter a new body or experience a new life. This process will no longer be necessary in the Age to come. You will leave whatever dimension you are currently experiencing, fully aware of who you are, what you have been and where you are going. You will evolve, or attain that new dimensional awareness fully intact, fully functioning in the present, past and future. Or, to be more accurate, you will be aware of who you were, who you are and who you will be. That is the important awareness.

To die a slow and torturous death, to see a loved one die painfully or suddenly, to see a child taken in their early years of golden promise, has been one of humankind's greatest tragedies, sorrows and most important lessons.

The medical profession is trying to continue life at all costs and often for the wrong reasons. At the other extreme are those who are advocating doctor-assisted suicide. Both of

these concepts are of a third-dimensional mentality and will fall by the wayside in the times fast approaching.

Life should be cherished as a joyous time of active purpose and fulfillment. Humanity should be taught from the beginning that at the proper time, there will be a graduation into the next level of awareness and higher attainment. This should be anticipated and honored as part of the perfect process of evolvement. All people should value their physical structure as an honored vessel, as a gift from the Creator, and treat it with care and respect. Each soul has its own timetable, its own agenda, and you must come to realize that everyone did not come to earth to live to an old age. If every soul lived their life in its fullness and close to Spirit, they would know when their time on earth was drawing to a close, when their mission was complete. They would gently and lovingly prepare for their transition, allowing those they love and cherish to be a part of the process. No painful disease would have to be experienced, no complicated and painful life-extension processes would be initiated, for each of you would know, without a doubt, when it was time to go forward, to evolve.

Your loved ones would know that the separation is only temporary, that each of you has your own destiny to follow, that one day you will be reunited, never again to feel the pain of separation. Native Americans and other cultures of the past who lived and died close to Spirit accepted life and death as the wholeness of experience on earth. They cherished life, but they also honored death. Age was also honored and revered, for this was the time of wisdom. One of the greatest tragedies of your time is the practice of placing your aged ones in isolated care centers where they are drugged or made to feel like worthless invalids and left to slowly perish in pain, loneliness and futility.

These concepts, practices and beliefs are ones that will soon be obsolete, and you will look back on them as barbaric. Age will be measured in experience and wisdom. Your bodies will mature, but not decay. Your minds will stay active, alert and ever seeking new experience and knowledge and when it is time for you to move on to the next level of the never ending spiral toward perfection, it will be done consciously, with anticipation and joy. This is beyond your conceptual abilities at this time.

The first step will be to teach the young to view life in a different way, as a precious gift and an opportunity to attain abilities and wisdom for the next level of experience. They must be taught that they are divine agents or representatives of the Creator and that what they do, positive or negative, affects not only their present life, but their future lives, as well as the rest of humanity, their spiritual family and the universe. This sounds like a tall order, but if the teachings were begun and instilled at birth, and perpetuated throughout life, what a miraculous leap in consciousness this would be for humankind!

We are not saying that you should not mourn your lost loved ones, but we do ask that you begin to view the process in a different light. First of all, they are not lost, and their passing is not without purpose. Anyone who places the responsibility for his total happiness, well-being and reason for living on another individual is inviting tragedy or separation. Your responsibility and greatest lesson at this time is to realize that you alone, in unison with Spirit, are responsible for you feelings of love, self-worth and fulfillment.

Have you not wondered why some mourn a lost one for years and never seem to get over the loss, and others mourn

for a brief time and then begin to get back in the swing of life and find ways to fill the void? Does this mean that some love more greatly than others? No, it usually means that either they have a need to martyr themselves, or that they do not feel they have the knowledge, ability or wherewithal to rely on themselves or the desire to take responsibility for their happiness and reason for living. They externalize, limit and restrict themselves from becoming fully conscious masters of their own destiny.

We ask you, dear ones, to begin to contemplate, restructure and reevaluate your old concepts of living and dying. This, too, is part of the transformational process. You must experience each and every facet of life in the physical until you have balanced and harmonized the process in its entirety. Then and only then will it be possible to transcend the death process, and to ascend into your Light bodies and spiral your awareness into those glorious new dimensions where death is only an ancient dream.

Those of you who have aged loved ones or those in the process of dying, give them and yourself a gift of sharing love, sharing insight, and participating in the experience, not ignoring it, hoping it will vanish. Be there with them in the process, and do what you can to smooth the way. Relive joyous memories, use your love, your healing touch, and call on Spirit to help ease the pain and to allow a gentle peaceful transition. You will be amazed at the difference it will make.

For those of you who have lost or will lose children or young ones, know that they came to give you joy, to teach you an important lesson that you needed to confront, or to simply bless you with their existence. Know that they are blessed, wise ones who will be there to show you the way

and, together, you will be reunited with your spiritual family. Their birth was not in vain, nor was their death. One day you will know the perfect plan and see the reason why it had to be.

Know, dear ones, that God does not punish. Know that everything transpiring now, seemingly bad or good, is all part of the plan, and part of the experience needed by humankind to advance to the next level of awareness. Judge not, either yourself or others. Allow each day to unfold in its perfectness, knowing that soon the pain of separation will only be a memory in the past.

You cannot see us, but we are here; you cannot see your departed loved ones, but they are also near. Tap into your higher awareness and connect with your Divine Presence and, we promise, you will never feel lonely or alone again. You are surrounded by loved ones in far vaster numbers than you can ever imagine. As always, you are loved, guided and protected. I, Archangel Michael, bring you these truths.

18. Message of Hope

What I wish to impart to you today is a message of hope and a glimpse of the future. I will begin by saying that it will seem for many of you as if you are experiencing a dark night of the soul, not only personally, but those around you, in your cities, country and indeed the world.

This does not sound like a message of hope, does it? But it is, for what you are all experiencing on a personal level, as well as a global level, is a clearing of negative forces or energy. Any area that is not of the Light, or vibrating at the higher frequencies of electromagnetic energy that is permeating your earth and solar system, will have to experience this cleansing process.

Those of you, and you know who you are, who have worked so diligently, loyally and lovingly, who know yourselves to be among the workers of Light, are wondering why. Why me? Why now? I thought I had eliminated all the negative influences in my life. I thought I was through with all the turmoil of the third dimension. And yet, here you are experiencing physical distress or discomfort, or possibly even dire illness, or you are experiencing conflict in your relationships, hardship in the workplace, or even threat to your security or abundance. Why?

This is the message of hope that we wish to bring to you. You have been told that miracles are in the offing, and this is true. You have been told that Light will shine in every dark corner, every crevice, every mind before the end of your century or the year 2000. In order for the Light to transmute the darkness there must be a clearing process. It is easy to say, "I give myself to the Light. I give all I am and all I own to the higher cause." But what happens when your security

is threatened? Do you scream and lament, "It is not fair! What have I done to deserve this?" When you or a loved one becomes ill, do you fall into despair and forget to call on your higher source and the miraculous gifts of healing that have been given you and others? Do you turn to the Comforter, the gift of your Mighty I AM Presence and the Violet Transmuting Flame?

Please make it the latter, dear ones. For then, you will have the power and assistance of the Heavenly Host behind you. Many of you are experiencing the last, residual clearing of disharmony, or let us say, experiencing your final tests before you are allowed to begin the process of ascending into a fifth-dimensional reality.

Oh, dear ones, there are such marvelous gifts awaiting you. Did you think there would not be a price? That you would not be asked to show through your faith and determination that you are ready for the gift of mastership?

The forces of Light are beginning to overcome and outshine the forces of darkness and negativity. But this is not accomplished without a fight, without distress, without turmoil, without sacrifice, without diligence, perseverance and dedication. Do not become faint of heart at this late date, my beloved warriors...not when you are so close to realizing and achieving all you have striven for since ages or aeons long past. You are so near, so close to reaching the goal...so close to realizing victory.

Accept the final challenge or challenges with joy. Meet them head and heart straight on with your spiritual armor strong and shining around you. Know that you have all the assistance, guidance and support that you will allow. By this we mean do not let your fear take hold and restrict you;

do not let your emotional body run amok and create a negative force field around you so that we cannot penetrate it and bring to you healing energy, purifying life force and transmuting, balancing, harmonizing vibrations to carry you through your trials. We are ready and anxious to help you make the transition as gentle and painless as possible. But it is all up to you. It is your decision. Will you help us to create miracles out of chaos for you?

It is the same on a national level and worldwide level. Do you not feel the anguish and suffering permeating the ethers that humanity has created for humanity? It cannot be allowed to continue. Small inroads, small efforts are being made, but much, much more is needed. It seems as though in some areas of your world there is no hope, no future—but this is not so. There is hope as long as there are those of you who are willing to stay true to your calling, to stay focused on your purpose and create a vibrational force field that will surround, enfold and permeate your earth.

There are those dear souls, many who are even now making their transition, or their exit from the earth, to dwell in other worlds and dimensions, and it behooves you to bless them and send them lovingly on their journey to the Light. There will be many more, and this too is part of the perfect plan. Be assured that we will care for them; they are our concern, not yours. It is those who are reaching for their truth, for that higher awareness, that sparkling glimpse of the future that are your concern...those who are ready and capable of making the transition to the next level of evolution and yet stay on earth and accompany her in her spiraling, thrilling journey closer to the great Central Sun and the God Force. It is for these that we ask you to be an example and an inspiration...to blaze a pathway of Light and love for them to follow.

And so, again we say, we bring you good news, glad tidings. You are not alone in your endeavors. Never again do you have to function in ignorance and darkness. As you transmute and release each imperfect part of yourself and your world, as you resolve each issue, as you balance and harmonize yourself and join with your perfect Higher Self, never again will you have to experience those painful events. They are resolved and gone forever, never to return. It will become easier each time you step out in faith and determination and meet the challenges head on because you will see how easy it is to walk through them with grace and beauty, leaving a trail of shimmering perfection in your wake. This is what existing in the fifth dimension means, dear ones. You will continue to grow, learn and evolve, but without the pain and anguish that you have experienced in your limited third-dimensional world. When you attain that state, you will live in beauty and harmony with yourself and all humanity, and your progress will continue because you will know that each step taken, each sacrifice made, leads to a reward beyond measure.

To walk in the Light among the Masters and to see the angels at work and at play, to remove your blinders and view all the wonders of Heaven...this is your goal. Is the struggle not worth it?

We give you our promise to walk beside you during your trials, to give you all the loving assistance that you will allow. Open your hearts and minds to us, beloveds; our goal is the same as yours, to be reunited. You are loved and protected by the mighty Angelic Forces, all the Lords of Light and the Masters. I AM Archangel Michael.

19. Create Your Perfect Reality

Beloved children of Light, I, Archangel Michael, come to you at this time to offer a challenge. I challenge you to put us of the Heavenly Host and spirit realms to the test, and I also challenge you to put your own mastership to the test.

You have read, listened, heard and tried to absorb and live all that has come to you from the many and varied sources. You have been told but you have not realized that it is, indeed, a time of fast-moving change: perilous, traumatic and disconcerting. Time and events test your faith, your stamina and your very soul. We have told you, time and time again, that you do not have to experience alone, without assistance, the transformation and transition; the times of seeming darkness and the whirlwinds of conflict that must transpire to make way for the lighter, higher frequencies of the new consciousness to emerge. And so this is my challenge to you:

I challenge you to put us to the test: to accept the outrageous concept that you are a co-creator of the new Heaven on earth; that yes, you are a Master, a master with all your seeming imperfections, but nevertheless a mighty master of all the creative forces of the God Mind.

I ask you to begin to create your new, perfect fifth-dimensional reality now, and how do you do this (or become conscious of the fact that you are already creating your reality in each and every moment)?

First, begin with yourself. For one week, just one short week, concentrate totally on yourself. Does this seem strange, selfish, or self-serving? My dear ones, how can you build a perfect world for yourself and those around you until you have a perfect you to experience that heavenly place? Imagine

in the greatest detail exactly how you would like to look, feel, move and think. Make it as real as possible. Experience this vision with all your senses. Feel the joy, the excitement. Imagine through your mind's eye the perfect you, and with your inner hearing, how you will sound.

Every time your mind strays to something else or moves into doubt, gently bring it back with an affirmation such as "I am now manifesting my perfect God Self" or "I Am the Mighty, Perfect I AM Presence—I AM a Christ of God." Live and breathe with all your essence this perfect beingness you are becoming. Awaken with the image before you and spend every spare moment of the day (instead of in needless wanderings of the mind) in concerted concentration on your perfect self in body, mind and Spirit.

Before you sleep, ask your perfect etheric double to join your physical, mental and emotional selves in manifesting this perfection so that it will continue the task throughout your sleeping hours (with even more power and effectiveness because your doubting conscious brain will be at rest). At the end of one week, affirm your perfection and then allow it to rest within. Allow it to build in power in the ethers, joining with like vibrations so that it will begin to manifest in the physical.

At that time, you will begin the next phase of perfecting your domain and, therefore, of co-creating heaven on earth. Place your concentration on your abundance or on your relationships or on your creativity, whichever area is most out of balance in your reality. Begin to build the paradise in which you wish to reside. Picture it in all its beauty, serenity and perfection. Build it piece by piece, brick by brick or stone by stone. Is it high on a mountain top? Is it on a peaceful shore

beside a placid lake or overlooking the ever-changing massiveness of the ocean? Are you in a community of enlivened, enlightened spiritual brothers and sisters, interacting, exchanging energies, love and inspiration, growing, creating together; or are you in peaceful, serene isolation, communing with the animal and spirit worlds?

Build this world, this paradise made to order, in all its perfection. Place in it or make room for those with whom you wish to share your world and feel it, sense its smells, sounds and solidness until it becomes as real (or more real) than the reality in which you now exist. Again, when your mind begins to wander, gently bring it back to this new world you are creating. When you feel stress, go to a quiet place in your paradise and sense the change—no stress or negativity allowed there. (It is paradise, remember?)

Create it down to its finest detail and see your perfected self walking, living, loving, existing in this heaven on earth. As with your perfect self, spend every spare moment concentrating on your creation: on awakening, throughout the day, as often as possible and especially before falling asleep. Again, after one week affirm your creation and turn it over to your Higher Self.

Proceed to concentrate on the next item of importance in your perfected world. If it is relationships, place each person according to his or her importance in your consciousness and imagine the perfect interaction between you. How would you act or interact with this person and how would that person respond? See yourself in perfect harmony with those around you: giving freely, accepting their uniqueness and complementing their talents and strengths with your own, instead of competing and striving for superiority and

supremacy. Feel the harmonious love and creative spirit flowing from one to another, magnifying, enhancing, until all of you become a unified spiritual force of love, balance and peaceful coexistence. Place your spiritual family in the paradise you have built and see it expand, grow and surround the earth until all is perfect.

You cannot build your perfect world without the abundance of the universe at your beck and call and so you must claim the truth that you are entitled to all the bounty and opulence created by the God Mind and know that it is unlimited in supply and available for the asking. You must create that certain, absolute knowledge within you that it is your heritage and God-given right to experience all perfection and abundance. And so for your next week in time, you must create, affirm and condition your being that this is so. How would it feel? What would you have? Consider not just your needs but your desires. Create it for yourself and for all those around you. Remember there is enough for all. Play with it and really seek within yourself to ascertain what is important to you. You may be surprised to find what you would really want in your world. You may not need all the gadgets, frills and fluff that are at this time considered signs of status and power. You might just possibly find that you would like to simplify your life and have the sleek, simple comforts, without having all the possessions that seem to own you and your time rather than the other way around. You may find that your priorities, the importance of things in your life, are changing to emphasize the beauty of nature and the purification of your lakes, streams and air, the time to enjoy the wonders of your world and to interact with the loving beings you have placed there.

You may find that all you want is simple, nourishing,

wholesome, satisfying foods, light foods that create and maintain the balance and harmony in your new perfected being. Your whole idea of abundance might change when you no longer feel you have to hoard, save and collect, surrounding yourselves with barriers to keep out intruders who might try to take your abundance away. When you make the startling realization that there is enough for all, you will relax. The realization must come from within and start with you so that it can radiate outward, building your perfect world, you see? Remember, as with the other visions of manifestation, spend one week in building this reality, analyzing, delving within, discarding old, outmoded concepts, half-truths, other people's ideas and expectations you have accepted as your own. Build your perfect abundance for one week, affirming throughout the day and night until you have firmly entrenched this idea deep within you. In other words, affirm abundance until you have accepted it as absolute truth.

Now imagine what you would do if you could do or be anything in the world. How would you fill your days? What would you create? What would you manifest in your world that would be the perfect example of who you are and what you stand for? You may not be able to quit your job as a clerk tomorrow and become a doctor or a teacher, but you can begin to see yourself as a creative force for change: a teacher, for example, of the new truth you are living; a nurturer of spirit and a healer for those around you, using all the gifts being offered you at this time. Allow your imagination to soar. Release your mind and feel the vision of the future. From the depths of your being, what do you want to be? What is your place in the New Age of Tomorrow that is almost here today?

Concepts and identities will change. Roles will be less

defined. In the times to come, none will be lower and none higher; all will be of the same importance, sacred and holy. You can be a server and a nurturer and consider yourself as important as a philosopher, doctor or scientist. And so, do you wish to be a writer, an artist, a healer, an inventor or explorer? What would you do if you could be any of those, or if you could manifest your wildest dream? What would you write? What would you paint? How would you heal? What is your concept? Even if it is outlandish and totally different from what is accepted now, build on this dream and make it as real and detailed as possible. How do you want to spend the rest of this life and the next, and the next? It should be your deepest soul's desire, for this is what you will get.

Remember, you are learning to co-create as an extension of the God Mind; therefore, we give you one admonishment: as you build and create this new reality, always, always be sure your desire is of the greatest wisdom and for the highest and best good of all, and complete your affirmations with "Thy will be done." If your desires are harmonious with those of your I AM Presence, all is well. If they are not, you are to place the desire of God before your own, for God's vision is perfect. Remember the saying, "Be careful what you ask for; you might get it."

Again, spend a full week thinking, concentrating, delving within, building this part of your reality until you are sure, without a doubt, that you know what it is you want to spend your creative energy and time on. What is it you want to be known for? What talents do you wish to claim as your own? Live, breathe, dream every moment until you can feel yourself becoming empowered with this creative energy and force. After a week's time, affirm it as truth beyond question and turn it over to your Higher Self.

After you have completed this process and firmly placed in your consciousness all you wish to bring into your world, stop and take stock of what has transpired, what has changed. Does your world seem somewhat different? Have you diverted your attention from all that is wrong with the world to the vast and wondrous possibilities available? Have your attitudes about people and possessions changed? Do you like yourself a little more? Do you feel more empowered, somewhat more in control of your destiny? You should.

What you are doing is focusing on what is right and available in the universe and what can be made manifest when you concentrate on becoming a co-creator with God for good, instead of being a helpless, ineffectual victim of circumstances (seemingly). These miracles will not transpire overnight but they will happen, especially if enough of you begin to accept your empowerment and the belief that you can build and manifest this heaven on earth in your lifetime.

After you have completed this process, I ask you to begin again. How has it changed from the first time? What would you add or what would you delete? It will become more refined and defined as you become more attuned to Spirit and more sure of yourself. It will evolve and change as surely as you will. Play with the process, enjoy it. Feel the thrill of manifesting. Know that you, too, can create worlds within worlds.

As you accept your masterhood and empowerment, we of the heavenly realms can infuse you with vaster amounts of life force and also redirect the cosmic energy of manifestation to you for your use. Can't you see that this is not possible until we know that you will use this energy for the good of all and not for limited, selfish reasons?

And so I ask you, I challenge you to begin—to join me and the Legions of Light in manifesting and transforming your beloved earth into the blazing star she is meant to be: a sparkling, pure, vibrant entity ready to join the galaxy and universe of which she is an integral part in her journey back to the great Central Sun of perfect unity and love. You are a shining star, you are a universe within a universe, you are perfection. All you have to do is reach out and claim your heritage.

It has been said that this year and the remaining years of this decade are times of great and tumultuous change, that the old ways will crumble and the Light and dark forces will battle for supremacy. We acknowledge that these predictions are true, but we tell you this: the dark forces are gradually being infused with Light and they do you a service by showing you what transpires when you choose limitation. The old must make way for the new and although it may seem like destruction and chaos, the phoenix will arise from the ashes and all will be born anew. Let the unenlightened continue as they will. Their turn will come in due time. Bless them, love them and know that the Spark of the God Force within them will not allow them to fail. They are just not ready to awaken. It is not yet their time. Know that you, as the Wayshowers, the Starseed, are blazing the trail for them to follow, and accept your full mantle of masterhood. You have come far and experienced much in the name of righteousness. Now is the time to accept who you really are, who you have always been: a Christ of God.

I, Archangel Michael, and all the Heavenly Host join you, support you and protect you as you accept the challenge of becoming co-creators of the new earth.

20. Welcome to the Gateway of the Higher Dimensions

Beloved children of Light, does it seem as if you are in a whirlwind of emotions, a swirling vortex of energy and about to step out into the abyss? Do you feel as though the boundaries and structures you have built for your security and comfort are crumbling? If so, we welcome you to the gateway of the higher dimensions.

As the negative energy is cleared from the lower astral planes of the fourth dimension, and as you become more centered and focused, enabling you to process more of the pure cosmic energy being sent forth, the veils of illusion are being lifted and dissolved for many of you. It may seem as if your reality is not as sharp and defined, but more fluid and nebulous, as your consciousness drifts in and out of several layers of parallel realities. It is as if you are learning to swim and are testing the waters before you take the great plunge.

We come to you at this time to assist you in the transition process, to help you step into the waves and currents of change so that you may flow effortlessly and buoyantly into the future. First we ask you to look at what is holding you back. What are the attachments and addictions to which you are still clinging? Where are you still rigid and firmly entrenched in third- and fourth-dimensional thinking and interaction? Are you addicted to being right, or maybe even being wrong? Are you addicted to the outcome of what you feel your new spiritual nature will or must be? Are you addicted to certain traditions or a particular set of rules and standards? Or are you addicted to power, or to being powerless? What attachments are keeping you stuck: relationships, possessions, a job, a certain identity, a particular location, your

physical body and whether it is healthy or unhealthy, or looks a certain way?

Many of you have been working diligently for a long time to bring yourselves into harmony of body, mind and Spirit. It is now time to let go and let yourselves be what your Spirit wants you to be. Do not be caught up in the struggle of the masses whether it be government, political, moral issues, or the actions of those around you. Allow, dear ones, allow your brothers and sisters to work out their own personal agenda and work through it in their own time frame. Each must walk his own path, and it is a solitary path—no one can walk it for him.

Those of you who have cleared the way, both physically and mentally, are now being sought out as high-powered conductors of energy and information. The vibrations are being turned up, you might say, so that it is difficult for those around you to not realize that something is going on—something that cannot be explained away by their rational minds and scientific means. And there are times when this energy seems almost too much to handle, even for those of you who have harmonized and prepared yourselves. You must learn to allow it to flow in and out freely. It will not affect you adversely as long as you stay centered and grounded and do not allow your mental processes to get in the way.

We understand that these are very stressful, uncertain times for all of you and that you are faced with many seemingly insurmountable situations. You would not be facing these situations, dear ones, if we did not think that you had the strength and heart to overcome them and prevail.

Envision yourself on a long path that stretches and winds upwards, a path that becomes more narrow as it reaches into

the heights and beyond your vision. See in your mind's eye how the path falls away on each side and there is nothing but darkness below. Now, do you walk slowly with your eyes cast down on the vastness below, or do you keep your eye fixed on the shining light ahead? It is important that you take one step firmly at a time, not focusing on your feet, but visualizing the goal before you. Anticipating the wonderful sense of accomplishment and the reward your victory will bring. This is the way we ask you to envision each day and each situation. Your Soul Self is placing before you that which you most need to address and resolve, but along with the challenge is all the assistance you require, if you will just call upon your I AM Presence and the wonderful guides and angels around you.

Do not let little setbacks discourage you, or make you falter in your faith. The negative forces like nothing better than to make you doubt or weaken your resolve. It is easy, precious ones, to say "I believe" when everything is going well and you are comfortable, but then you also become complacent. Unfortunately, in your physical world, strength of purpose and lessons are learned through trial and adversity.

We, too, have our challenges, and even though it is a different reality and there are different rules in the higher dimensions, it is also possible to coast or move forward at a slow pace, or take up the challenge and push forward. This is what being a Light warrior means, dear ones. You who are of my legions, are being called forth, being made ready for the "Big Event," and you must be prepared. You are in training, as you move through the initiation process, under the direction of your Higher Self and Divine Presence. So flex your spiritual muscles, firm up your spiritual resolve, overcome and lay to rest those residual challenges before you and clear

the decks for action, because the Call to Arms will soon go forth. What we mean is, it is time for you to take your spiritual stand and claim your masterhood. You must be ready to step forward.

And so, do not lament if your life is unsettled, while many of those steeped and entrenched in the third dimension seem to be moving blissfully along with their material rewards accumulating while they go merrily on their hedonistic way. All is not as it seems, and here is where you must not judge and feel as if they are being rewarded while you are being punished or chastised. This is far from the truth and this will soon be evident to you.

You, as the Pathfinders and the Wayshowers, must hack through the jungles of rigid thinking; you must dissolve the shackles of mass consciousness and break through the barriers of the third dimension so that the Light of the New Age can pour forth on humanity. We have not told you that it would be easy or comfortable, but you assured us, many ages ago, that you were up to the task and could handle the pressure and overcome all the obstacles. We took you at your word and we tell you this: even though at times you doubt yourselves, we never doubt you, our brave ones, we know what you are capable of and what you can accomplish. And so we ask you to keep your eyes on the victory and the shining future. Fill your hearts with the loving energy we send forth for your use. Talk with us in your meditations or your quiet times and we will answer. Oh, dear and faithful warriors, we are uniting and coming together in great and wondrous numbers. More and more of you are remembering your heritage and joining or connecting with your spiritual family and there is also a great gathering in the etheric realms as well. We are amassing our forces and girding ourselves

for the great task ahead, and we know we will be victorious.

You are needed; you are loved; you are each an integral part of the marvelous plan for the future of your earth and your solar system. Know that one day you, too, will be released from the confines of earth and the bonds of the third dimension, free to soar the universe on the wings of glory. And so, be of great courage and good cheer for your progress is awesome to behold. I, Archangel Michael, bring you these truths.

21. THE ME INSIDE

What can I do to prove to me that I am all
I'm meant to be?
What do I mean, what do I seem,
outside my eyes looking in?
I travel up and down life's road,
gliding, stumbling under my load,
On a path, smooth and free,
then on a detour where I should not be.
I clear my mind and my eyes, calm my heart,
see the disguise of promised
Thrills, worthless things,
all the pleasure success seems to bring.
Inward, onward, upward I go. I love life's dream,
but in my heart I know
There's more than this. I'm a visitor here,
what will I be when I disappear
Into another realm, another plane, who will I be,
what my name?
Will you be there, those I cherish so much?
Will I recognize you, or
Feel your touch? My love for you,
your love for me, more a treasure
Than any other can be.
I need the warmth of your heart on mine.
The shared love through all skeins of time,
most important will be,
You are there with me.

Ronna Herman

22. Embrace Your Physical Form— The Temple of Your Spirit

Greetings, beloved children of Light, how exciting and inspiring it is to witness the transformation that is taking place on your planet earth. As the waves of energy pour over you and permeate your inner being and that of your mother earth, miracles are beginning to happen. We, of the heavenly realms, see the Light that is growing stronger in and around you, and feel the vibratory rate that is rising into the ethers or astral planes, while you of the physical realm tend to see all the darkness and negativity that surround you. That is why we wish to assure you that you are making progress; you are making a difference.

Let us now speak to you of your bodily form, the vessel that houses your Spirit. All through the ages, you have had a love/hate relationship with your physical body. Many of you, upon accepting the challenge and the assignment to enter the third-dimensional plane of duality and participate in the experiment of a free will world, did not realize you would have to clothe your Spirit in a physical body. You imagined you would stay in your Light body and participate from a distance overseeing the experiment from afar. And so, when you were entrapped in the constricting confines of a physical form, you began to resist and struggle for release (when you could still remember from whence you came).

You gradually forgot as the veil of illusion and the restrictions of the physical world grew stronger, but you still held the memory within your cells of your true identity and the free spirit of your true nature. Thus began the struggle between the ego/desire body and your Spirit. Some of you unconsciously, over the ages, have subjected your body to great

harm and deprivation as a result of these memories. Time and time again, you sought release from your physical vessel only to be reborn anew to play out the dance of transformation.

The time has come, dear ones, for you to embrace your physical form for the beautiful vehicle it is. You are a keeper of great truth and knowledge, knowledge buried deep within your cells and throughout your being. You are a conductor of frequency, a transmitting station, a storehouse of vast information that you must recapture and reclaim so that you can assume your true identity and complete your earth mission. You must seek to balance and harmonize all parts of your being, realign and balance all misqualified energy and release the tentacles of darkness that have kept you captive in ignorance and limitation. You must seek to purify your body in thought, deed and habit. As you release the impacted energy and negativity from your cellular structure, it becomes lodged in other parts of your body, your blood stream, your organs, your glands and your bones. You must release these toxins and once again gain the health and vitality that is your heritage.

There are numerous ways to do this and much has been written about symptoms of the "mutating Light workers." We encourage you to listen to your own inner guidance and agree to follow the nudging of your Spirit whether it be a change in diet, fasting, body work, acupuncture, massage, or other forms of body alignment, breathing exercises and body movement, as well as toning, aromatherapy or crystal healing. All of these will help speed up the process of cleansing and aligning your physical, emotional and spiritual bodies and thereby increase your capacity to absorb the higher, more refined energy. Many of you do not realize that Light

energy works much the same as food energy—if your bodily form cannot process the energy and release it, it impacts in one way or another. This is the reason that many of you (who have had this ongoing love/hate relationship with your bodies) have put on weight during the process, especially in the area of the solar plexus, even though you may be eating less than ever before. Light is energy and must be expended. You are mutating very quickly, dear ones; you are learning—growing through experimentation.

Those who have become comfortable in their bodily form, and have made friends with this wonderful vessel, have had an easier time in the transformational process for they are not at odds with their physical being and are not constantly battling for supremacy over it as though it is something to be conquered.

Each part and parcel of your being is an integral part of the whole and must be accepted for its beauty and its contribution to the whole. All must be brought into harmony and balance, and as long as you must function on the physical plane, you have need for your physical body.

The Light energy that enters your body is activating and energizing coded Light crystals that were placed there aeons ago when you first came to this solar system. They have lain dormant, but are now being reactivated. New chakras or energy vortices are also being activated so that you will eventually have twelve major chakras and the double helix of DNA is being added to until you will once again have twelve strands of DNA (now manifesting in your etheric body). This is what will initiate the transformation of your physical form, along with the infusion of Light, building your vibrant, youthful, ageless, ascension body.

You are growing more powerful and vital every day, my beautiful ones, even as you struggle through your growing pains. Accept every challenge and opportunity to release old impacted energies. Remember what transforms inwardly must also manifest outwardly in your physical reality. This is why so many of you are experiencing so many conflicting situations in your daily lives. Do not hide or try to avoid these challenges, we implore you. They have come forth so that, once and for all, you can resolve all disharmony, all imbalance, both within and without. This is why it is so important that you solicit the help of your guides and teachers and all the angelic beings who are so ready to serve and assist, that you stay focused on your highest intent, and that you look to the rewards to be attained rather than the discomfort along the way.

You have been encouraged to build your future, your bright new future, day by day, moment by moment. This is most important, as the energy waves increase and the turmoil around you grows. You must stay focused, centered, surrounded in the glow of loving protection of pure Cosmic-consciousness so that the maelstrom of negativity and misqualified energy cannot affect you.

Simplify your lives, dear ones. Concentrate on what is permanent and lasting. Become an assimilator of truth, love and knowledge instead of collectors of material goods and seekers of short-lived physical pleasure. Bring your world into balance, peace and harmony, and all good things will come to you. However, you may find that you have different priorities, different habits and tastes.

You are making inroads on healing your mother earth, but not nearly enough, nor quickly enough. More must be

done and soon. We plead with you—TAKE HEED! It is time to resume full stewardship as guardians of the earth, as protectors of the species that have been placed here in your care. It is time for you to assume your true identity as Masters of Light, as keepers of peace and conveyers of truth and love. Do not miss this opportunity, dear ones; do not abort your mission and have to climb through the ages of darkness again as you did after the downfall of the Golden Ages of the past. The bells of the Ages are tolling and the transformation of your species waits for no one. Either you accept the gift and go forward or you fall back and continue in the cycles of darkness, strife, ignorance and limitation. The choice is yours.

Come forward, dear ones; reach inward and upward. We extend to you our symbolic hand of Light, the gift of the Creator and Life. We await your return. You are needed; you have been missed. I, Archangel Michael, and the Heavenly Host surround you in love and protection. And remember, you are never alone.

23. Angel Food for the Mutating Starkind

(Researched by Ronna Herman and validated by Lord Michael.)

Drink the purest water you can find; even some of the so-called purified water or spring water has harmful chemicals or elements in it. Buy the best water-filtering system you can afford or have the water you drink tested for purity. Occasionally, you might want to add some beneficial minerals to your water—you can buy these in pure, concentrated form and add a few drops according to the directions. You may also add a crystal or different colored stones to your pitcher of water and this will help to energize and harmonize it, making it more beneficial. Also, drink water cool or room temperature, not cold. Drink at least six to eight glasses of water a day. Try to break the coffee and soda habit. There are so many good herbal teas out with no caffeine, but nothing beats pure water.

Safflower and olive oil are the most beneficial oils for the body and small amounts should be used every day (not heated to high degree).

Celery and apples are good for balancing the acid/alkaline ratio of our bodies. Carrot juice is great for cleansing. A combination of carrot and celery juice, alternated with apple juice (diluted with a little water, if you wish), is very beneficial for a one to three-day fast, very effective for releasing toxins and impacted energy.

You may feel hungry for the first twenty-four hours, but will feel invigorated and full of energy after the first day. Many of us have deep-seated memories of starving in past lifetimes and this is a good way to break the pattern of thinking you

will die or become ill if you do not eat for a few days. This happened to me and it was a great breakthrough.

A good cleansing and rejuvenating diet (also to lose weight):

Each day have four to six veggies, two fruits, one starch, one protein, and one slice whole grain (preferably sprouted) bread. Do not drink with meals; drink fifteen minutes before and one hour after but not during. Be sure to drink six to eight glasses of water, or more, to flush out the toxins.

Almonds are a great alkaline food, you should have at least 8 to 10 a day, no skins if possible, and raw. Do not eat too many, however, as they are high in fat content.

Do not eat white flour or sugar; instead use rye flour, brown rice, millet, yellow corn meal, honey or natural maple syrup or fruit juices. These are non-mucus-forming and best for weight loss and stabilization.

Soups are wonderful, filling, tasty and economical. The best I have found are: vegetable, onion, split pea, potato, barley and mushroom, or experiment and make up your own combinations. Learn to use a minimum of salt; you can retrain your taste buds over a short period of time. Instead use creatively the wonderful combinations of herbs such as Mrs. Dash and the great assortment of herbal seasonings available. You soon will not miss the heavily salted food and artificial seasonings, and your taste buds will begin to enjoy the subtle taste of natural foods.

Cayenne pepper used in capsules or sparingly on foods is good for increasing the metabolism and, believe it or not, is good for the stomach.

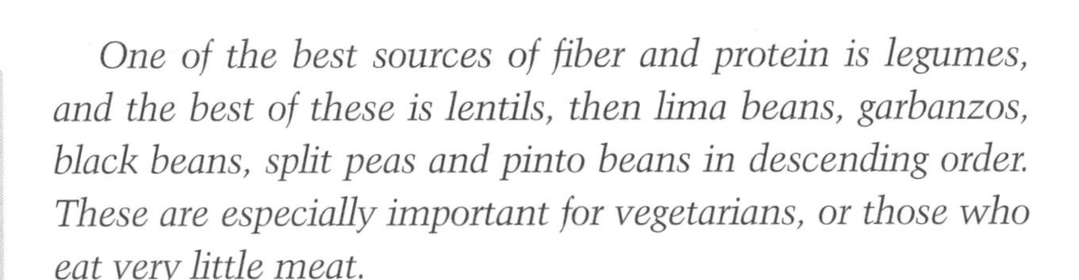

One of the best sources of fiber and protein is legumes, and the best of these is lentils, then lima beans, garbanzos, black beans, split peas and pinto beans in descending order. These are especially important for vegetarians, or those who eat very little meat.

Beets and the beet greens are great for cleansing the liver and gall bladder. Beet juice is also good, but only sip small amounts.

Carrots, beets, string beans, zucchini, peas and squash are very beneficial and high in "Light" nutrients. Lightly steam, I prefer to not use the microwave.

At least once a day, eat a large salad with several kinds of dark greens (very little iceberg lettuce should be used), three or four raw veggies of various kinds, different kinds of sprouts, a few raw sunflower, pumpkin or sesame seeds and a few chopped or slivered almonds. Use a light dressing of olive oil and lemon or seasoned rice vinegar and spices of your choice.

Bananas, potatoes, & hubbard squash are very alkaline and great for balancing the acid/alkaline ratio in the body. CHLOROPHYLL is a good blood builder and oxygenator.

We need to balance our ration of sodium and potassium. Sodium is the most third-dimensional of the elements used in nutrition, or "time" elements as labeled by U.S. Anderson in his book The Greatest Power in the Universe, *while potassium is one of the most "space" elements. Space elements in food convert to energy, while the time elements convert to substance.*

Cosmic energy has the same effect on the body as energy from food sources. If we take too much in and expend too little, we increase our bodily weight. We must learn to run

the forces of cosmic energy through and back out of our bodies, in a circle (or a spiral), so that they do not impact and imbalance our bodily form. There must be a free-flowing circuitry; that is why it is so important to clear all the blockages in your energy vortices or chakras.

Our Higher Self or Christ Self is in charge of overseeing how we utilize energy, and the more evolved we become, the more sensitive we are to the food and energy we ingest. It is our higher consciousness' way of gently nudging us to remember what we have forgotten and to return to the pure, natural lifestyle of our ancient beginnings here on earth. We walked this earth as magnificent, perfect, powerful Light-beings and this is the state to which we are returning. Any imbalances and discomfort are signals from our Higher Self to our body that a particular area or some detail of our lifestyle needs attention and changing.

We must always be gentle with ourselves and not make hasty judgments or condemnation. Ask your Magic I AM Presence and your Higher Self to give you the desire and will to make the changes necessary for your optimum health and well-being. Use the Violet Transmuting Flame daily to speed up the process of eliminating the toxins, habits and desires that no longer serve you.

Each day claim your perfection and ask Spirit to guide you through the day in perfect balance, peace and harmony and then listen; you will be guided toward your perfection. See you there, dear friends.

24. The Divine Sword

Beloved children of Light, I wish to share with you, in part, what transpired at the wondrous gathering, the celebration and reunion of Lightworkers, called the Conclave of Michael, in Banff, Alberta, Canada on March 24-27, 1994.

Many of you are aware that this is the location of my etheric retreat, the place where in those golden days of perfection on your earth, I, along with other angelic beings, as well as the Masters, the devas and elementals were visible to you. We walked, talked and interacted with you. We did not appear as solid or clearly defined as you do now, but then neither were you before your descent into the lower dimensions.

You all are anxious and desirous of seeing and communing with the beings of the higher dimensions, or unseen realms, but what you have forgotten is that we have walked among you in the past and we were as real to you at that time as you are now to your friends on the material plane of the third dimension. Some of you are gaining an awareness of this and it will become more apparent as time passes.

We have held many of these conclaves down through the ages and they have always been during times of great transition and momentous change in the history of your world. This gathering was no exception. What transpired can rightly be called an introduction to the fifth dimension, for many of those in attendance reached levels of awareness, unity of purpose and feelings of oneness never before experienced in this age of human existence.

If only I could show you the magnificent thought-forms that rose from the vicinity of the conclave, the powerful feelings of love, the exquisite colors and the strength of the energy that was emitted via toning, meditations, powerful mental interactions brought forth for peaceful and harmonious purposes, and the unerring dedication to the highest cause, you would never, ever doubt the power and strength you have at your beck and call. Your world and all the beings in its close proximity benefitted more than you will ever know from the unified, synergistic action of this most holy, blessed group.

This was a gathering of many of the masters of your future, those who have dedicated themselves and all they hold dear to the cause of transformation and ascension—the building of the new Golden Age. Every area of human endeavor, every facet of disunity and disharmony was examined, discussed, and valid, viable conclusions and processes brought forth. There was no struggle or vying for superiority or leadership; all walked in their integrity, sharing their wisdom and seeking the knowledge and experience of all others to add to and enhance their knowledge and effectiveness. It was a reuniting of a spiritual family unit, a bringing together of all the myriad facets of awareness, the bringing of gifts to share and to add to and complement the whole.

The gifts of love and awareness, the feeling of oneness and unity felt at this gathering was just a precursor of what is to come as you all begin the process of reuniting with the whole which will culminate in an awareness and unity with the rest of your fellow travelers in other dimensions and the Godparents of your universe, your Father/Mother/God who reside in the Great Central Sun. This is your destiny, your ultimate goal.

I would have you know, in part, what was transmitted by me through this channel at this conference. First of all, you

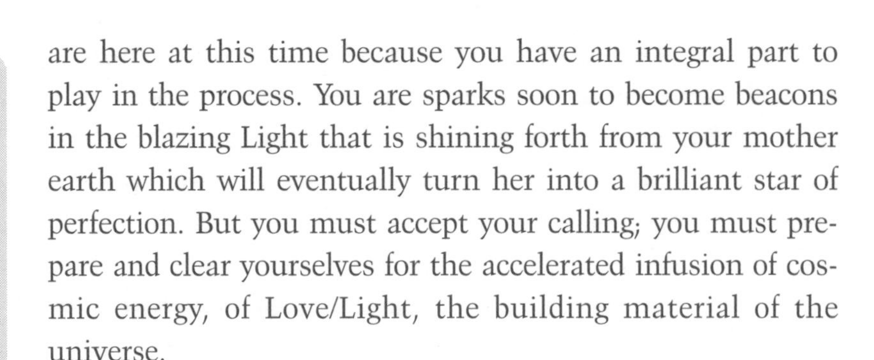

are here at this time because you have an integral part to play in the process. You are sparks soon to become beacons in the blazing Light that is shining forth from your mother earth which will eventually turn her into a brilliant star of perfection. But you must accept your calling; you must prepare and clear yourselves for the accelerated infusion of cosmic energy, of Love/Light, the building material of the universe.

No longer will this energy be sent down in a blanketing effect to cover all your earth and all humanity indiscriminately. You can see the devastating results of the negative use of this blessed energy: those who hate become more hateful; the obsessive strive for more power and dominance; the greedy seek more and more wealth and possessions, no matter what the cost or how much pain and anguish it causes others; the senseless annihilation of your brothers and sisters is really destroying a part of yourselves.

Now, the energy of love and Light will be withdrawn and focused, like a laser beam, on those of you who have cleared and balanced your physical, mental and emotional bodies so that you can be loving, effective conductors or facilitators of this energy, magnetizing it to you, energizing it through you and then, projecting it out from you in a total loving, compassionate way for the highest good of all humanity. You are surrendering your personal agenda for the magnificent cosmic plan of evolution and reunification with the galactic hierarchy and the return to your rightful place in the cosmic order. And it will be focused on those areas that will eventually be the shining cities of Light, leaving those countries and areas dark with hate and fear to struggle and eventually grow weak and perish from lack of the life-giving force of the Creator.

Along with this gift of enhanced and focused energy comes an admonition: you must take this energy and put it into action. You must move forward and begin the process of becoming a wielder of power with purpose, in harmony with the divine plan. For if you do not, the cosmic gift of creation will be withdrawn from you and it will be focused on another who will use this cosmic energy for its proper purpose. Even if they are not as prepared as you or as talented as you, to those who use the gifts bestowed, more will be added until they are empowered beyond all imagination. The time for contemplation and theorizing is over, for time as you know it is running out. It is time to claim your heritage, to step forth into that role and task that only you can fulfill...the task you accepted before you came into this world of the physical.

It was also said that these are to be the days of miracles. Possibly small, insignificant ones at first, but as you claim and acknowledge these miracles, larger manifestations and more miraculous events will be forthcoming. Hold out your hands and your hearts and let them be filled to overflowing with the abundance of the universe: loving relationships, peace, joy and harmony, and yes, an abundance of material wealth so that you can show the world how a master lives in that rarefied dimension beyond the third density.

Dear ones, make every effort to join together in meditation, prayer and purposeful action. Share your dreams and aspirations, and support each other in your chosen endeavors. It is the time of unity, cooperation and gathering together to act in unison to show the world what can be accomplished when there is a conspiracy of lofty ideals...a divine agenda being put into action by powerful masters for the benefit of all humanity, not just the few.

You know that I bear the Sword of Divine Will, Truth and Valor, but did you know that symbolically this sword was placed in your right hand while you were still in the etheric realms as one of my appointed warriors in my Legions of Light? However, you have not always used this sword as it was intended. Down through the ages it became a sword of power for the masculine energy and a symbol of dominance, conquest and war. I will not take this sword from you, for you have great need of divine will, truth and valor, but I would temper its use and give you a new weapon. After you read these words, my blessed warriors, go inward and sense the truth of what I say and feel the energy course through you so you know that, indeed, this gift is being given to you.

Center your consciousness in your crown chakra and feel the petals of this vast energy source open wide. Envision that silver cord, which grows wider and stronger every day, reaching upwards toward your Higher or Divine Self. Now sense and envision a blazing sword of blue Light, with a center of white and gold crystalline energy emanating from it slowly descending and piercing your crown chakra and travelling down your spine, energizing and enlivening each of your energy centers or chakras on the way. Feel it as it pierces your root chakra and firmly implants itself about two feet into your earth mother.

Experience the blaze of electrifying energy that surges forth, surrounding you, creating your spiritual armor which nothing of lesser energy can penetrate. Envision the hilt of this sword nestled at your heart center; see the Threefold Flame burning brightly within, for this is your spiritual insignia. This is the insignia you carry on your shield of valor. Stretch your arms wide and see implanted in your left hand a blazing gem of blue for divine will. In your heart's center see a

shimmering sun of golden energy begin to glow as your divine wisdom is activated. Anchoring the sword in your right hand is a gem of iridescent pink for divine love. We are changing the polarities of the masculine and feminine sides of your body so that you can fuse these energies and become more androgenous, more balanced, more unified.

This is not the cross of crucifixion, my beloved ones, but the sword of resurrection and ascension. This is the feminine sword that I place within each of you to temper the masculine sword of power with the compassion of love and wisdom. This is the sword you will wield as you go forth on your chosen mission.

I have told you again and again that these are the times of reunification, of coming together. But first you must become reacquainted and reunited with all the myriad parts of yourself as one so that you will bring wholeness as your gift to the changing mass consciousness. It is a step-by-step process, you see? Therefore, you have been instructed to see to your own spiritual health and well-being first. You will find that once this is accomplished you can forget about your personal growth or enlightenment, for you will have reconnected with that powerful, perfect part of your being. Then, and only then, will you truly be prepared to serve the greater cause. You will no longer be in a state of becoming, but a state of BEING. You will be your spirituality, your truth, your integrity—a being who emanates the perfection of the Christ-consciousness. This is your goal, and you are not as far from it as you might think, my dear ones.

There was an inspired infusion of the divine love force instilled in all those who attended this conclave and the power of this infusion will resonate throughout the world.

Each of you will feel as if you are being fine-tuned or more closely directed toward that which you are to accomplish—your individual part in the plan or mission. So, dear ones, we ask you to stay tuned to that divine station of your heart and soul, for the message is one you will not want to miss.

I have placed my sword of love and compassion within your being and I also have strengthened the connection between you and your Christ-consciousness, dear ones. Go forward with the assurance that you are being divinely guided and the rewards of your labor will soon be realized. I, Archangel Michael, bring you these truths.

It was said at the Conclave:

"DO NOT JUST WALK YOUR TALK, BUT FLY YOUR VISION!"

25. Manifest the Dream

Beloved children of Light, let us take you into the future for a glimpse of what is to come, for a picture of what you have to look forward to after all in your lives has been brought into balance and the cleansing process comes to a completion.

We understand that you are weary, sometimes discouraged and often frustrated. But we would have you know that it is all for a purpose, a higher purpose, in which all humankind will benefit. No sacrifice, however great or small, ever goes unnoticed. All are duly noted and recorded so that the rewards you will reap from your dedication and steadfastness can be returned a thousandfold.

We have assured you that in the times to come, you, who have worked so diligently and have, indeed, suffered through a dark night of the soul in order to bring the many parts of yourself into harmony, will begin to see the miracles of your faith start to manifest in the realm of materiality. Your path of destiny will become more clear and defined and the way will be opened to you, as obstacles fall by the wayside. Your health and relationships will improve and the disharmony that still remains in your immediate world will begin to evaporate as resistance seems to melt away.

Dreams and visions will begin to clarify and come into sharp focus so that you can move forward, creating them in solid, physical form, thereby manifesting your new reality, showing those who doubt that what you have been saying all along is, indeed, true.

Prepare to streamline your life, dear ones. Discard that which no longer serves you; eliminate the extra baggage of

possessions that, in truth, are more in possession of you—your time, your energy, your attention. Make way for the new mode of living, that of a close-knit community where those of like mind, heart and intention will be drawn together to support, assist, nurture and strengthen each and every part of the whole, no matter how small.

The energy that has been poured down upon your earth indiscriminately until recently will now begin to be focused in certain areas. Each of you, those who are attuned and ready, will be irrevocably drawn to that area which resonates with your Soul Song, the echo of perfection that you have carried down through the ages, buried deep within your cellular structure.

Over the next few years as the energy in these areas intensifies, miracles will begin to manifest. Buildings, services, homes, schools, streamlined and efficient; all things needed to be self-sufficient will appear with ease. Beauty, balance and harmony will be the key words and by this we mean that nothing will be sacrificed or neglected. Mother earth and nature will be a major consideration in the planning, as well as the addressing of all the needs of the people—they will not be in conflict, but harmonious and nurturing.

Those who do not resonate with these higher vibrations will not feel comfortable in these places; therefore, you will not have to worry about anyone settling there who is not in attunement. They will have no desire to remain for they will feel a distinct discomfort, not knowing why but, nevertheless, very obvious to them.

The areas of distress will continue to be so until, either by cataclysm or assistance in cleansing via the energy and power of the Light warriors, the beings involved begin the

process of awakening and start to take control of their own destiny. Day by day, you are growing more powerful, dear ones, and the dynamics of your focused intent is being felt around the world.

As leaders, the miracles that you are beginning to manifest will make many of the doubters start to notice that something is truly happening, that it is not all just "airy-fairy, hocus-pocus." They will begin to acknowledge that you are making things happen. You are creating harmony in your lives and all around you. You are peaceful and serene, and none of the turmoil that is going on in the consciousness of the masses seems to touch or impact upon you.

Ah, then you will see; they will come to you and begin to ask questions. How is it that you have accomplished all this so easily? (Of course, little do they know.) What is it that you are doing that is so different? What is it you know that they don't? And you will tell them that they must turn inward and how they, too, can begin to draw on the power of the universe.

Do you not see the barriers that are being broken, not just physical structures, but belief systems? The issue of health care, treatment and the importance of preventive maintenance for the body has taken on whole new dimensions. Allopathic physicians are being forced to look at the antiquated methods they have so stubbornly clung to for ages. Balance and harmony of body, mind and spirit are becoming normal statements for the masses, not just New Age gurus.

No matter how much those of a third-dimensional mentality resist, the barriers of race, creed and culture are slowly being dissolved. The time of isolation and self-interest is coming to a close. The time for the motto of "All for ONE and ONE

for All" is beginning to creep into the common consciousness.

Transition and change always create feelings of uncertainty and anxiety. But we tell you this, dear ones, all the changes that you allow to happen with the intent of highest and best good for all will ultimately bring about all the dreams and desires you have carried internally for so long, manifesting as your "Brave New World" of peace, joy and abundance.

Let those around you see the strength of your faith, the value of your determination and your unswerving dedication to your purpose. It is time to speak out, dear ones, and declare your intent, not to preach, but lovingly and assertively expressing your true feelings: who you are, what you stand for and what your vision is for the future of the earth and its people as opposed to the doomsayers and those with an anti-everything attitude who think they know the truth and keep themselves and all those around them wrapped in a cloak of pain, fear and negativity.

So, we ask you to go forth each day, determined to live each moment in serenity and in assurance of the perfection to come, fortified and surrounded by your mighty I AM Presence. Affirm that "For this day, I will trust the inner voice of my Christ-consciousness, and I know each step I take and each task I perform is only bringing me closer to the dream I hold so close to my heart."

All of you, dear and precious warriors, with your loving energy, and with our help, will support and lift the earth and its inhabitants up to the next level of awareness and into a new consciousness. We will not fail, dear ones, not this time: you have the assurance of all beloved beings of the heavens. We enfold you in an auric field of love and protection. I AM Archangel Michael.

26. The Pillar of Spirit and the Cross of Matter

Beloved Masters of Light, I bring you greetings from the Most High. We have spoken of the sword of ascension and we have spoken of the cross of resurrection; now let us delve into the cross of Spirit and matter. You descended on the Ray of Light that was your connection to your Christ Self, or your I AM Presence, which was the vertical energy pillar of Light, but as you moved down into the third-dimensional experience, the realm of the physical, you became anchored by the horizontal pillar of matter, forming a cross.

As you became more dense and steeped in matter, the Light pillar of your Higher Self shrank until it was a thin, narrow cord, while the horizontal pillar of matter grew heavier and grosser. These energies are anchored in your heart or soul center, the center of your being, and as you became out of balance in the polarities of the physical, a seesaw effect began. First tilting heavily to the right and then to the left, back and forth, you see, always keeping you out of balance, off kilter.

That process is now being reversed: the horizontal cross member that is keeping you anchored in the physical is shrinking, narrowing and becoming shorter in length, while the pillar of the I AM is widening, becoming stronger, blazing forth as more and more of your Christ Self is being accessed. This is the symbology of the cross and why Jesus, the Beloved, was crucified on a cross. His resurrection was the triumphant victory of Spirit over matter.

And that is the process you are experiencing now, only you will not have to die on the cross; you will transcend the cross, and ascend on the pillar of Light.

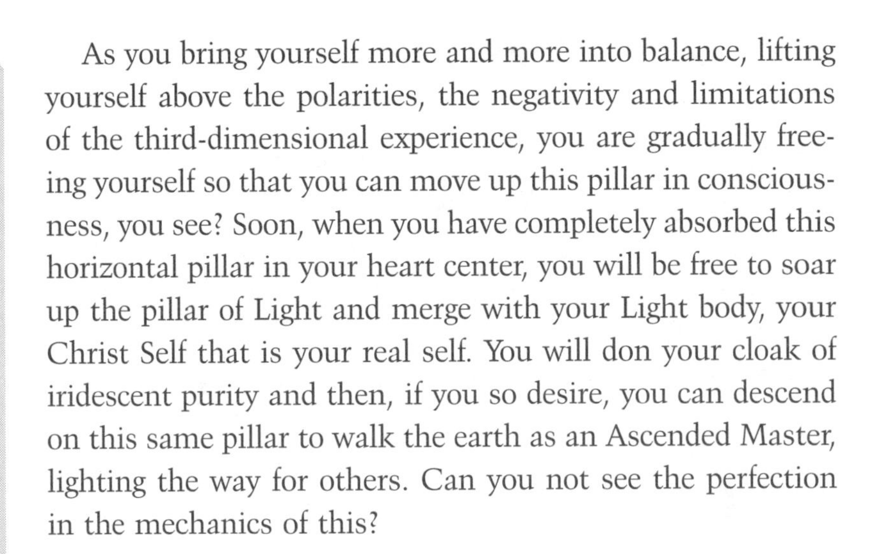

As you bring yourself more and more into balance, lifting yourself above the polarities, the negativity and limitations of the third-dimensional experience, you are gradually freeing yourself so that you can move up this pillar in consciousness, you see? Soon, when you have completely absorbed this horizontal pillar in your heart center, you will be free to soar up the pillar of Light and merge with your Light body, your Christ Self that is your real self. You will don your cloak of iridescent purity and then, if you so desire, you can descend on this same pillar to walk the earth as an Ascended Master, lighting the way for others. Can you not see the perfection in the mechanics of this?

All of you have your eyes directed toward the heavens, looking for signs and portents of what is to come and we tell you this: there is no greater show in the heavens than the one that is manifesting on your planet earth right now as soul after soul bursts into enlightenment and awareness. As more and more of you access the energies of manifestation in the higher fourth dimension in preparation to enter the wondrous harmonics of the fifth dimension, we will be able to assist you in realizing your dreams, your ambitions, your desires, not only for your own good, but for the good of humanity and your solar system. We can send you the electromagnetic energy of the God Mind into the third dimension, but we cannot bring into manifestation that which you desire. That is your task, that is why you are in the third-dimensional experience. Only when you begin to access the higher realms of finer vibrations can we assist you, empower you in your endeavors.

So many of you are lamenting that you have prayed, meditated, affirmed abundance, good health, etc. but to no avail. Until you bring this cross of matter into balance, and you

are able to raise your consciousness up along that pathway to your real self to access the treasures of manifestation that await you, you will not attain your desires, or they will manifest slowly through much effort.

See yourselves as perfect; see your trials and problems for what they are, illusion or misapplication of energy or thought. We have told you that you must begin to see your world from the vantage point of a Master, and by that we mean that you must see all in balance and harmony. When you bring that pillar of material consciousness back into its proper place, in your heart center, your soul will burst forth in a blazing golden light of awareness, power, truth and purity.

Do you not realize that although you are anchored to the core of your earth now and you had to be to enable you to live out this experience of duality, you were originally anchored to the core of perfection, the Great Central Sun in the heart of your Father/Mother/Creator? You are still anchored there, but the tug and pull of the third dimension has stretched that connection to the breaking point. You must release the stress and strain on your soul, dear ones. Keep your feet anchored on the earth for the time that remains, but release your Soul and Spirit to soar back up that Light pathway on which you descended.

As you become more balanced, releasing the polarities in your life, you are also releasing the earth from the stress and strain of the tug and pull of polarity. When you become a totally empowered Light-being, the magnificent energy of the Christ-consciousness will flow, nay, pour down in great streams through you into the earth. Then, dear ones, you will see the miracles of the New Age come forth.

You must come to realize while you are still in this experience of the third-dimensional limitation that all points of view have an equal right to be, that for someone they are valid. You do not have to agree or condone, but they are in existence because of the lessons some of humanity must experience. Do not give the thought-forms of the lower vibrations power and strength by resisting them, hating them, fighting them. Free them through love with your higher knowledge and the Transmuting Violet Flame. Walk in your power and your truth, but know that it is not your place to change anyone's mind or make him over into your image.

If you are totally surrounded and filled with the Light of the Christ energy, none of the negativity that is swirling around you will affect you. To the contrary, you will affect it by being who and what you are. Bless the misinformed, comfort the downtrodden, pray for and see whole all those who still labor and suffer within the prison of their negative thought-forms. You are making a difference, beloved Masters. The lower astral planes are slowly being cleansed of all the misqualified energy of the ages, allowing more and more pure Light to filter down on your world. As you strengthen this pillar of your I AM Presence, more of the pure Christ energy can be focused on you as a bearer of Light, as a master of co-creation.

In your meditations, see this cross of matter shrinking, becoming smaller and dissolving into your heart center. See yourself rising up on a pillar of golden white Light to meet us, to join us in the rarefied worlds of the higher realms. See the cross of matter shrinking around the world, releasing your earth and all humanity, so all that remains are great white shafts of Light coming down from the heavens piercing each and every heart and your planet until all is a glowing beacon

of light shining out into the universe, declaring the birth of a new star, the earth.

First must come the recognition of what is out of balance and what is not of the highest wisdom, dear ones; then must come the restructuring, the corrections, sometimes even through destruction, clearing the way; and then comes the resolution, the soul-u-tions, the rectification, or the resurrection into the higher form, the form of truth, unity and balance. That is the path you are on, the task that is before you.

Use the power of the crystal pyramid in your meditations to access the etheric world of your Christ Self. Here you bring yourself closer to the realm of manifestation and empowerment. Know that, as you consciously build this vision in your mind, you are building these crystal pyramids in the etheric, and that one day soon, they will be manifested on your North American continent, in the Light cities of the future. They will be the foci of cosmic energy from the Universal Mind, the places of enlightenment, healing and wisdom. Build these light cities in your minds as you envision your new world for here will manifest many of the miracles of your future.

Guard and monitor your thoughts, dear ones, for they are powerful as you are powerful. Do not add to the imbalances of your world, but concentrate on bringing yourselves into balance and then helping your brothers and sisters to harmonize and create unity and peace both within and without.

Create such an aura of peace and harmony around yourselves that everywhere you go you will spread the Light of perfection and leave in your wake the glow of pure Love/Light.

We are assisting you in every way possible, dear ones, and look forward to that day when your consciousness will be

balanced enough to reach up and touch ours so that we can infuse you with the gift of pure awareness, pure en-lighten-ment. That is the day we envision happening soon. Keep trying, dear ones; you will not fail. We are greatly pleased with your progress. I, Archangel Michael, and the Heavenly Host salute you.

27. The Clock of Life

The clock of life is wound but once,
And no man has the power
To tell just when the hands will stop,
At a late or early hour.
Now is the only time you own.
Live, love and toil with a will.
Do not wait until tomorrow,
For the clock may then be still.

Ronna Herman

28. Breaking Agreements— Releasing Outmoded Concepts

Beloved children of Light, I, Archangel Michael, speak to each of you who reads this as if we were in direct communication with each other, for indeed we are. You who resonate to my name, my image, my words are being called forth to claim your identity—your affiliation with me and my Legions—your heritage.

You must begin by accepting responsibility for the world you have created and then earnestly strive to rectify and balance all the imperfections around you. It is time for you to release all the outmoded, outdated, false concepts, the half-truths and untruths that you have allowed to rule you for these many ages past. It is time for you to break all the agreements you have made with all the other parts or fragments of yourself. Dissolve all the karmic ties and agreements you have made, release all the restrictive, binding imprints that have been placed upon your soul, or your etheric body, since your first incarnation on the physical plane. These are sometimes referred to as dark or light crystals, imprints and implants or encodings, but no matter what they are called, it is time to fill yourself with Light, which is true knowledge, the wisdom of the God Mind.

You can begin by becoming aware of all the different kinds of agreements you have made and lovingly release yourself from them, and release any other person involved as well. This includes any agreements made with entities on the astral plane which are retarding your growth as well as theirs. Begin by writing out your personal list of any and all agreements you wish to break. Make this list as long and detailed as necessary. Meditate on each item and try to feel the core and cause. In other words, allow your Higher Self to guide you through the meditation until you feel you have reached an understanding as to its source and then infuse it with the Violet Flame of Transmutation, releasing yourself and anyone else involved. Rescind the agreement in its totality, past, present and future and send all of its energy to the Light to be transmuted into perfection.

This may take some work and some time and it will involve your participation in active meditation, or communion with your Higher Self, your guides and teachers. The benefit will be two-fold: you will clear the way for a greater infusion of pure cosmic energy, thereby bringing your bodily vehicles into more perfect alignment, and you will also build an active working relationship with your guides and teachers. The results will be transforming and, seemingly, miraculous. Be prepared to spend as much time as necessary on each agreement until you feel a completion. Also be prepared for your relationships to change and evolve. As you release the restrictive agreements from yourself and others, realize that some relationships will probably end. Allow the transitions to take place in your ways of being, thinking and interacting with others.

The first step to growth is the awareness that something needs to be changed. The next step is having the courage and will to make the necessary changes. This is the basis of the ascension process, dear ones. Releasing the restrictive, limiting third-dimensional energies that bind you and replacing them with the empowering, unlimited, loving vibrations of the higher fourth and fifth dimensions.

After you have worked through the process of reprogramming your mental and emotional natures, releasing the old restrictions, it is time to build and construct a new vision of

your greater, expanded self...the masterful co-creator that you are destined to be—that for which you are now in apprenticeship. We gave you a challenge a short time ago, a way to build your external world and manifest what you want in your perfect world on the physical plane. Now we ask you to build and strengthen that vision as to how you will function in this world by releasing all those energies that no longer serve you. This will help you more perfectly define who you are, what you will be, how you feel and what you will do in this perfect new world. You must build a world that is to be shared with all others; for the highest good and benefit of all, there can be no selfish desires included here. There is enough abundance, bounty, joy, love, peace, pleasure and comfort for all humanity if you would all just take off the blinders of limitation, selfishness, greed and fear.

You must build an inner circle for your vision. Carefully, meticulously, in the most careful detail visualize and express in written form what your vision is for yourself; who you are, how you will feel and interact with others; what you will be and do. State in detail what you wish to accomplish during the rest of your time on this physical plane, a road map, your long-term game plan. Decide and define who you will need to help you accomplish this plan. Do not place names or faces in the plan, just attributes and let the universe supply those who are most harmonious with your vision. You are setting the stage to draw forth your soul family—your perfect counterparts—the fragments of your vaster self. We have promised that you will no longer have to strive or struggle alone and this is the fulfillment of that promise, but we must ask you to clear the way for the perfect energies, the perfect souls to enter your consciousness and your inner circle.

We then ask you to extend your vision to your outer circle, or the world at large, again, creating a wider circle of influence. How do you envision it? What is your part in it? How does it fit in with the greater whole? By this we mean, what will your group and inner circle contribute to your community, state, country, the world, the solar system, etc. All must be in harmony for the transformation and transmutation into the higher octaves as your earth spirals into the fifth dimension and your solar system, galaxy and universe evolve to the next higher rung of attunement with the Great Central Sun.

It would also be helpful if you would utilize the great healing tool of harmonics, or toning, as you seek to break these agreements. If you are not familiar with the term or process, there are numerous tapes and explanations as to how this is done. The basic principle is that of releasing impacted energies via sound. Allow yourself to experiment with loud sounds (not screaming): release your breath with a loud, sharp POW sound, chant AUM or OM at various octaves, or even try loud moaning or sharp expulsions of sound which facilitate the release of impacted energy. We will not go into detail as to the process for there are many good sources available for this information, but be assured this is a useful and valid tool, one that will be utilized more and more, along with color and aromatherapy for balancing and healing the body/mind in this emerging New Age.

We ask you to open your mind, to expand your awareness and begin to utilize all the tools that are being offered you during this momentous time of change. As we have stated many times before, begin to join together to create a synergy and cooperative effort to accomplish these healing and balancing tasks so that you do not have to struggle alone. The unity and dedication of purpose, the loving interaction

with like-minded people is one of the greatest gifts being offered you at this time. Do not stay isolated in pain and rejection. Know that there are those who have the same purpose as you, the same desires and goals. All you have to do is put out the call and make the effort and they will appear, one by one, as if by magic. Your loving vibrational intent will radiate the call and those of like vibration will feel it and be drawn to you.

The winds of change are blowing strong; the vibrational impact of planetary influences are creating shock waves throughout the planet earth. The earth is in the midst of her emotional cleansing as is evidenced by the great flooding taking place more frequently in your country and other areas of the world. Humanity is becoming more and more anxious and distressed by these energies and it is paramount that you seek to become balanced, harmonious and strong in spiritual awareness so that you can weather the times of uncertainty and the storms of change.

Allow yourselves to be lifted and carried on the waves of ascension, or the waves of spiritual enlightenment, the infiltration of Light within you which is spiritual wisdom, the permeation of Light around the world which will bring peace, love and unity among humankind. We of the celestial realms are here to serve and nurture you during this time of rebirth and transformation. I, Archangel Michael, offer my protection and guidance. Call and I will answer.

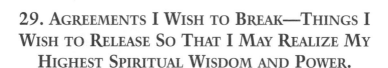

29. Agreements I Wish to Break—Things I Wish to Release So That I May Realize My Highest Spiritual Wisdom and Power.

I call upon my mighty I AM Presence to fill me with wisdom, discernment and loving intent. So it is!

1. I release any and all expectations I have about my spiritual growth and advancement. I will live each day in the moment, concentrating on bringing myself into harmony in body, mind and emotions with my Higher Self.

2. I release all agreements with my mother, my father, my children, my stepchildren, my husband/my wife, my brothers, my sisters, my friends, my ex-husband/my ex-wife or anyone else who keeps me stuck in a third-dimensional reality.

3. I release all invalid concepts about my worthiness of love, joy, peace, harmony, security, abundance, creativity, youthful vitality, health and well-being, aging and death.

4. I release the need to save the world or anyone in it. I realize my mission is to accept my masterhood and be a living, loving example to all without expectations from anyone.

5. I release all preconditioning and all cell-memories about my bodily form. I claim my God-given birthright of beauty, vitality, health and well-being, knowing that this is my natural state of being and I only have to follow the nudgings of Spirit to manifest this perfection.

6. I release all expectations regarding my creativity and work. I work and create for the joy of it and know that my abundance and resources come from Spirit and not from my efforts, only from my belief of my worthiness.

7. I release any and all hold that the third-dimensional government and establishment have over me. They do not control me or my abundance and security. I am totally empowered to manifest safety, be totally self-sufficient and totally in control of my destiny.

8. I release all residual karmic debts and misqualified energy within me and my physical, mental, emotional and astral bodies. I now resolve all conditions with grace and ease and expand into the Light in order to join in the co-creation of heaven on earth.

9. I release any misconceptions regarding my ability to draw knowledge, wisdom and pertinent information from Spirit and the higher realms. I draw forth new knowledge, concepts and wisdom in order to learn and grow and serve as a living example.

10. I release all judgment, all preconceived ideas and expectations for other people, knowing that they are in their own perfect place and evolvement. I give love and encouragement and only offer information when asked and then with the admonition that my truth may not be their truth.

AND SO IT IS!

30. Masters of Light

Beloved Masters, I, Archangel Michael, bring you greetings from the Most High. No longer will you be called "Children of Light" for many of you have outgrown that title or that level of your training. It is time for you to step out and claim your true identity, that of Masters of Light, warriors in the vast Legions of Light who have come to rescue this planet called earth and its inhabitants from the darkness and limitations of disunity. It is graduation time, dear ones, time to let go of the feelings of helplessness and aloneness, time to feel the surge of power from within you that is being supplied by your Higher Being which will help you feel the at-one-ness of all if you will allow it.

Release the little pictures of your reality, dear ones; begin to see yourself and your world from the vantage point of a master: the greater overview. You have investigated and delved into your past lives and experiences to better understand yourselves and to help in resolving residual issues of imbalance, but now it is time to release that small part of your great and extensive history. All of your experiences on earth were part of a growth process, an evolutionary process that was designed to prepare you for this time, the culmination of this particular experiment.

Let go of the little details and focus on the vaster drama unfolding. Look for the theme within your lives that will tell you what your part in the final drama of ascension is to be. Do not lament that you do not know where your destiny lies, or what your mission is. Your destiny is ascension; your mission is that which is being mirrored to you every day. Confront it, accept it, acknowledge it and it will swell and grow in your heart and awareness.

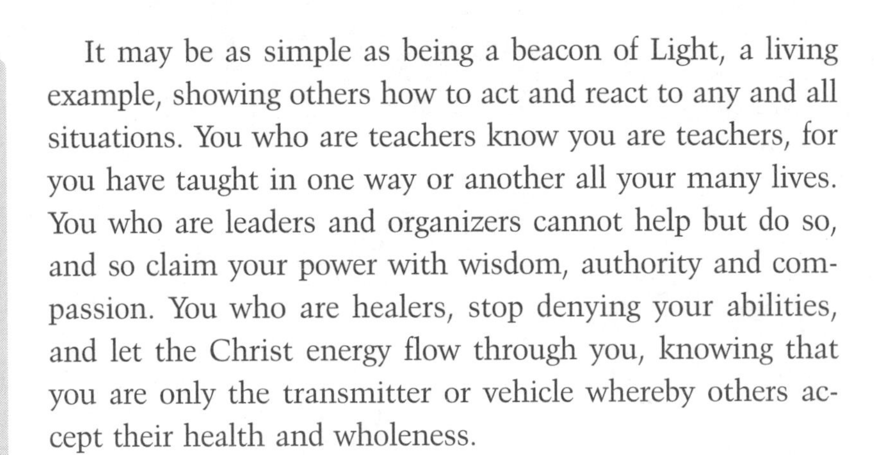

It may be as simple as being a beacon of Light, a living example, showing others how to act and react to any and all situations. You who are teachers know you are teachers, for you have taught in one way or another all your many lives. You who are leaders and organizers cannot help but do so, and so claim your power with wisdom, authority and compassion. You who are healers, stop denying your abilities, and let the Christ energy flow through you, knowing that you are only the transmitter or vehicle whereby others accept their health and wholeness.

Healers of the earth and those attuned to the devic kingdom are of vast importance and must begin to display to the world the magic they are capable of—that of bringing into balance and harmony the many elements of nature with humanity, coexisting for the highest benefit of all. You can place yourself in one of the four categories to begin with: is your focus of a physical, mental, emotional or spiritual nature? And from there is it a focus of integration, balance, expansion or elimination?

By now, you should realize that all these elements lead to the same place, awareness of who you are, which is a master in the process of ascension. It is time to stop judging anything or anyone as good or bad, as less or more. It is time to view your world and its events from the rarefied perspective, a higher-dimensional viewpoint from which you can see that all is perfect and each person is exactly where he needs to be, in the exact situation and circumstances for his greatest progress toward the Light.

You will be glad to know that we are taking a hand in many events, moving things along more quickly, you might say, and this is through the consent and cooperation of all of you, the vanguard, the Starseeds. Time is speeding up

(which is actually caused by the increased vibratory rate you and your earth are experiencing), and events are being compressed into a shorter time frame. So it may seem as though many more negative things are happening around you. But the results are that more and more people are beginning to realize that it is time to change; things are not the way they used to be. There is unrest, discontent, fear and a feeling of helplessness. This is where you step in to supply the answers, the example, the new awareness.

So do not despair that your world and humanity is sinking lower and is lost. To the contrary, beloved ones, you are on your way home. You are carrying the Light of the world on your shoulders and it is time to let it beam its great rays across the skies, around and through the earth.

It is time to bring the darkness into the Light, to balance the polarities of masculine and feminine energies, to focus on the Spark of the God Force in everyone and everything, beaming your Rays of Love/Light indiscriminately to all people and every situation. A Master sees perfection and Light in everyone and everything.

The Christ energy that is being sent to each of you who are masters cannot be requalified, dear ones. The Christ Light is information from the highest source and the Christ Love is the tool of manifestation in its highest form. It is sent down from the Throne of All That Is and filtered down to you through the Great Central Sun and the Hierarchy of the Heavenly Host. You, in turn, act as transducers and transmitters of this pure energy and wherever or whatever you focus your intent on is affected in the greatest possible way. It is "en-lightened" or transformed to the degree or level of its capacity to receive this pure energy.

On the other hand, the electromagnetic energy, or the "stuff" of manifestation that is used to create worlds, is malleable or changeable, according to the vibratory rate of the user and the free will of the user. Do you see the difference? So do not be afraid that you will increase the energy or power of a negative force when you send it the Christ Light. To the contrary, dear ones, you are performing a great service for you are loving it free; you are releasing it from the bonds of darkness. And when enough of you begin to focus the Christ Light on the dark areas of your world and solar system—yes, even Lucifer and his angels, they will have to relent and accept the Light. They will not be able to resist. God intends for ALL his creation to return to the Light, not just part of it. Is it so hard to accept the premise that the Father/Mother/God is capable of transforming and receiving all their creations back into their heart, the place from whence we all came, no matter what we are now?

Let go of the fear, beloved ones. Sense the perfectness of the plan: the great separation, the journey out into the far reaches of the farthest universe, the feelings of despair and futility turned into a feeling of hope and a new vision as you are inexorably drawn back into harmony with your galaxy, universe and ultimately reunited with the All That Is.

We are all on the same journey, dear ones. Come, join hands with us and let's make the journey together. I, Archangel Michael, bring you these glad tidings.

31. The Angelic Realms Will Become More Real and Appear to You More Often in the Glorious Days to Come

Beloved Masters of Light, I wish you to sense my presence, to know that I am not somewhere "out there," but just a dimension away, interacting with you and infusing you with love and protection, if you will allow me to do so. And so for just a moment, close your eyes and see if you can sense the warm, soothing flow of the Creator's love that I am transmitting to you. You may feel a tingling, or a feeling of expansion, or just a mellow sense of well-being, but make no judgments, just allow. We want you to begin to feel with your extrasensory perception, your true feeling nature, and not be ruled by your ego's emotional nature. We want you to begin to accept the concept that there can be heaven on earth and that you can walk among the angels and the Masters. You have before and the time is fast approaching when it will again be possible.

It is time for you to tune into the healing, vibrant tones of the higher frequencies. These are tones you cannot hear with your three-dimensional physical ears, except perhaps once in a while when you get a high frequency ringing in your ears. But as you come more into balance in your four lower bodies, you will become sensitive to these higher frequencies of sound and color.

As you and your earth begin to experience more and more of the fourth- and fifth-density refinement, moving up through the different planes and levels, you will be exposed to what you might call unusual phenomena, but in truth, it is much more normal than the illusion in which you have existed for so many ages. This is why we are now able to

interact with you more easily. This is why there are more appearances by the angelic forces around the world and why it is being brought into the consciousness of humanity.

Do you not see the perfectness of this? First, in the mid-eighties, there was a renewed interest in the angelic realm. Many of you began to study and investigate, stimulated by a strong desire to know more about the higher dimensions. You began to invite us to be a part of your meditations and to have an active part in your daily lives, thereby giving us permission to make our presence known. And now you are seeing the results. There are angels everywhere; pictures, statues, postcards, angel books, movies and stories about angelic rescues and intervention abound, and sightings or visitation are becoming almost commonplace. And so you see what a change your perception has created.

First of all, your earth has moved into a fourth-dimensional frequency, making it possible for us to interact with you again. This was difficult when you were in the third-dimensional fog and density. You also gave us permission via your free will, thereby allowing our interaction and joyous participation.

The veil of illusion is growing thin and even dissolving for many of you. You are beginning to realize that you do not have to suffer, that the Creator never intended for you to live in agony or feel pain. You are beginning to get a glimpse of how vast creation is and how awesome and powerful you really are. You are gaining a new conception of what the material realm is all about and that you have choices as to what you will experience, that pain and struggle are caused by fear of change and the unknown. You are beginning to come into the awareness that you are not on this physical

plane just to acquire "things"—material wealth and possession—and that you must struggle to get your share because there is not enough to go around.

You came to anchor Spirit in the physical, to bring under Spirit's control the emotional and mental bodies, to experience the solidness and joy of co-creating on the material plane, thereby allowing the Creator to experience physicality. But as the ages passed and you sank deeper into density, you began to believe the illusion that the physical existence was the real world, the real you. Nothing could be further from the truth, dear ones. You are a spirit, a Spark of the Divine Creator, in a physical structure, not the other way around. What is happening now is that you are being brought back into awareness and alignment with this truth.

As you go through these next months, please be aware that all the adjustments you are going through, the physical discomforts, are bringing you back into alignment with your true self, preparing the way for the reemergence into your magnificent Spiritual Self, a Christed-being residing in a physical form. Allow the imbalances, emotions and waves of sadness to flow through you freely, thereby releasing old memories, impacted energies, negativity and harmful beliefs that no longer serve you. Be gentle with your mates and friends and support them in their times of vulnerability, just as you must ask for their support and nonjudgment in your times of stress. We are all in this together, my precious ones. All creation is moving into a new level of awareness in unison.

You might question what you or the earth can do to assist us of the higher realms in our evolvement. Never mistake how important you are and how vital it is for humanity

and the earth to join in the progression of the universe back toward the perfection of the Creator. The experiment on earth has been a grand one and much has been learned and added to the universal consciousness. You are brave and bold, and your efforts have not gone unnoticed. You have accomplished more than was ever thought possible in these last fifty years of your time. As you move higher on the evolutionary scale, you will add a new dimension of awareness, a new refinement to the emotional and mental nature of creation, and a new understanding of love in the physical expression.

And so we ask you to begin to sense our presence, to open your minds to the wonderful possibility that we can appear to you or among you, that we are not somewhere far distant but we are here beside you as you begin to tap into the higher planes of experience. We are anticipating more and more of you opening or clearing the pathways for cosmic telepathic interaction. What a grand experience that will be for us to be able to communicate with you on a regular basis and for you to be able to tap into different informational sources at will! As you lift your consciousness, you will be able to access more of the great wisdom and truths of creation. That is why so much new information is being brought forth at this time. But would it not be better if you could go inward and tap into these sources yourself? The feeling nature of direct communication and the interaction of the experience will move you quickly past many of your old barriers and belief systems into new realms of possibility.

The rest of your year is a time of clearing and releasing the old residual energies, beliefs and restrictions that no longer serve you and are keeping you imprisoned in the third-dimensional experience. We encourage you to step out of the mold that has you imprisoned, to be daring enough to reach

up and out and embrace the divinity and sovereignty that is being offered to you. You will not be sorry, dear ones. No, indeed, you will wonder why you ever hesitated and how you existed so long in the pain and limitation of your old world. The illusion is fading away...allow the new vistas, the new world of tomorrow to emerge in your consciousness so that you can bring it to fruition, into full manifestation as quickly as possible.

It is time, my valiant warriors, and we are here beside you to give you encouragement, guidance and direction, and most of all, to bring into your awareness the great love we and all Creation have for you. I, Archangel Michael, bring you these truths.

32. You Are the Higher Self of the Fragments You Have Created

Beloved Masters of Light, I bring you greetings from the Most High. Let us continue our lessons with regard to Spirit and matter, only this time we will speak in terms of the power of your thought-forms and the expressions of energy you have created down through the ages through your powers of manifestation.

Just as you are fragments of a vaster Oversoul which is, in turn, an individualized portion of a much greater Being of Light—each created to manifest and experience, thereby gaining wisdom and destined to eventually be reintegrated back into the magnificence of the All That Is—so have you created fragments of yourself through your own experiments with the energies of creation.

Through trial and error, while steeped in the third-dimensional density, you have fragmented your Soul Self, building extensions of yourself which you may wish to call entities, who are attached to you via threads of energy and reside in either higher or lower dimensions, depending on the frequencies of the energy you have fed them. This is partially what is meant when we say you have many parallel selves or lives on parallel dimensions.

Now, you are being told that all is being brought together, reconnected, rejoined into itself on the way back to the more refined levels of energy or creation. Therefore, these parts of yourself, whether harmonious or not, are being brought into your experience, sometimes creating great joy and new awareness, but most often creating discomfort and imbalance. We have heard many of you lament, "Why must it be so difficult to be a Light worker? We are trying so hard; why must there be so many challenges and obstacles put in our path?"

We tell you this: first of all, since time as you know it is speeding up so much, what would normally take lifetimes is happening in days and months. Since you are being reunited with the myriad parts of yourself, whether that part is steeped in the belief of lack and poverty, unworthiness or lack of love, thereby failing to draw to you worthwhile or loving relationships, denial of creative abilities, or in being powerless and at the mercy of others; whether it is belief in violence and the battle with the dark forces, or in ill health and the inevitability of the aging process and ultimate death—regardless, you are being brought face to face with all the facets of your Soul Self.

It is inevitable; it is the path to masterhood and ascension, but we can help you to integrate these parts of yourself with more ease and grace. We can give you the means and wisdom to confront these issues from a higher vantage point, from the viewpoint of a master. You can "love" all those imperfect parts of yourself free. You can balance them before they are brought into your energy field for harmonization and reintegration.

This is the process we wish to give you to help ease the way through this transition process: Place yourself in a meditative state; we suggest that you might want to use a crystal to magnify the energy field around you and to enhance the energy being focused through your crown chakra. Call in your guides and teachers, the Masters and your I AM Presence, as well as enfold yourself in the Violet Transmuting Flame. When you have completed your invocation, project your consciousness out into these other parallel frequencies. See these entities you have created—you should know what and who

they are; every area in your life that is not in balance, that is causing friction, pain or keeping you off balance, out of the flow with your Higher Self, is created by an energy you have given life to down through the ages.

Now some of the energies are very powerful. If you are strongly addicted in some way and cannot seem to break the addiction, this is because you have given so much energy to this being and it will do no good to fight or struggle against it. You will only feed it more energy and strengthen it by doing this. How many times have you been told, that which you fear or struggle against, you empower or draw to you? Make these energies real—see them, identify them, acknowledge them. You have tried to ignore them for so long, pretending that they do not exist, but this does not work, for eventually you validate them by yearning, via strong emotional energies, for a cessation of what they create in your life.

At times you feel you are not in control of your life and this is true, dear ones. You will not be in control until you have integrated these fragments of yourself and reunited their energies with your Soul Self.

After you have identified these various energies or entities, begin to feel the power of the Christ energy glowing in your heart center like a great golden Sun. Feel this energy grow and build until it permeates your entire body and your force field or aura. Then begin to project this energy toward each of these entities, in turn, filling them with golden light, Love/Light, until they are transformed. You may have to do this with each entity several times if they are especially empowered, but when you feel you have balanced and neutralized their energies, see them being drawn toward you on a stream of Light. If they are balanced, you will draw them

into your heart center and integrate them there, feeling a great sense of peace and release.

If they are not ready to be integrated or still hold some residual, misqualified energy, the entity will stop at some point and not enter your force field of Light for they cannot penetrate this protective barrier you have placed around yourself until they are also of pure Light. This is how you will know that there is more work to be done.

In this way, my brave ones, you will not suffer or be so distressed during these tumultuous times of transition.

While you cannot integrate with your Higher Self or Christ Self until you are balanced and vibrating at a higher frequency, you can use your new-found powers to control the reabsorption of your own fractured energies. We ask you to begin to make use of these gifts for there is no time to waste. You will either integrate these parts of yourself with ease and grace, or through trial and tribulation, but they will have to be integrated. This is the evolutionary process you are in the midst of: the ascension process first focuses on reunification, balancing and harmonizing of energies, and then frequency acceleration. You have asked for ease and grace and so we offer you these tools to facilitate a more graceful and smooth process of transition.

As you become more sensitive and the veils between dimensions become thinner, you will find yourselves slipping in and out of the various realities, thereby manifesting the highs and lows, the mood swings and the disconcerting impulses. Many of you have blamed these on the dark forces, but believe me when I tell you, dear ones, it is not the dark forces at play here. It is all those parts of yourself that are crying for attention for they are feeling the impulse and desire

for reunification, just as you are. So acknowledge them, validate them. It will not make them stronger; it will open the way for loving interaction and reintegration, not for more stress and strain for recognition.

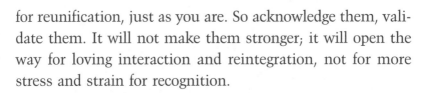

Just as you are straining toward your Higher Self for love and wisdom and the power to reunite, so are they. YOU ARE THEIR HIGHER SELF, you see?

And so on and on it goes, up the ladder of evolution, up the spiral of awareness, inexorably drawing all the many parts of the God Mind slowly back toward itself. The Great Inbreath has begun, my beloved ones. You can make the journey kicking and screaming, resisting all the way, or you can catch the wave of ascension and ride the crest, maybe a little frightened by the height and the unknown, but exhilarated and joyous, knowing you are in the arms of the Father/Mother/Creator after all, and so nothing can harm you.

Make your peace with yourselves, dear ones; then come and join us for the ride of the Ages. You'll never be sorry. I, Archangel Michael, make you this promise, and so it is.

33. The Pathway of Light

Beloved Masters, I bring you greetings from the Most High. I have an important message to deliver to you, brothers and sisters of the Light, an update, you might say. As we have often told you in the past, it is very difficult to predict what will happen next in your corner of the galaxy as events and changes are occurring at an unprecedented rate. However, as a major goal is reached or, spiritually as you move through another initiation or higher level of consciousness, we can forecast what is likely to happen next in the realm of physical reality.

This year of 1994 has been a year of momentous change, both in the structures of your physical world and in the expansion of your spiritual awareness. Boundaries of countries and nations are changing; ethnic groups are changing places, either by choice or by force; many dear souls are choosing to transcend, and believe us when we say they are moving on to a more harmonious place and better conditions. Bless them in their choice, for their Spirit Self certainly knows what is best for them. Humanity is becoming more and more restless, for nothing is as it was, and what could be counted on before is no longer stable or available. The weather patterns are so erratic that droughts shrivel crops and shrink water resources in many areas, while great storms send deluges of water to others, creating untold misery and loss of resources.

Patterns and boundaries of every kind are changing and shifting, mostly brought about by the changing patterns of human consciousness. As the higher frequencies anchor firmly in your world, both in your consciousness and that of your mother earth, great pressures are building. These frequencies are much finer, more subtle, but they are also much

stronger, you see? Just as darkness must give way to Light, so must the lower vibratory energy waves give way to the higher, more refined frequencies.

Awesome in its magnificence, the Love/Light energy from the highest source in your universe, the Creator/God/Goddess, is being anchored on your earth and is now available to you. A great energy highway, so to speak, has been opened from the Creator Source to you, if you are ready and willing to open yourself to this miracle.

But make no mistake; this is energy that is so dynamic, so profound, you must be a balanced, harmonized receptacle, firmly anchored in your Soul center, free of ego and personality restraints.

This energy also comes with a caveat: "Accept this gift from the Source only if you are ready to surrender to your highest calling and are willing to serve as a master of co-creation in transforming the darkness of your solar system into Light. And you must be ready to join your galactic family in its accelerated evolutionary process; you must expand your vision to include not only your earth and your solar system, but your galaxy. You are coming out of isolation, out of your narrow, tunnel-vision point of view. You must realize, once and for all, that you are not alone in the universe. What affects you affects all of humanity, and what affects your earth affects the universe."

This is a year of clearing and cleansing in preparation for the even greater changes soon to come. Those of you who are diligently working to clear all negative energy patterns within your multiple energy bodies, who are striving to bring balance and harmony into your consciousness and your surroundings, will have a much easier time of it as these

momentous changes begin to come about. You will be well prepared for what is to transpire in the near future. You have built a strong, firm framework for yourselves so that not only can you be of service, but you will be ready to reap the marvelous rewards that are forthcoming via new gifts of awareness, abilities heretofore unheard of and almost instant manifestation of your dreams and aspirations.

Much new mind-boggling information is coming forth almost too fast to assimilate. Some of it seems to contradict what you have heard in the past and many of you are quite confused. It is not that the information given over the past 2000 years was not true, dear ones, but the knowledge that was brought forth was kept at a very basic level that humanity could understand and absorb. You can see how the teachings of our beloved Jesus have been distorted and misapplied, and even many of the supposed New Age truths have been distorted by those who have brought forth information which was not always from the highest source, though this was usually with the best of intentions.

So you see, as your awareness increases, as your purity of mind and spirit expands, so do your abilities to absorb vaster, more complex information. This is not only the beginning of a New Age, but you, as spiritual beings in human clothing, are coming of age.

As you open the pathways to higher and higher dimensions and remove the static that has kept us out of touch for so many ages, you will receive clearer messages, more profound information, more information that is entirely new to you, more vital statistics about the universe in which you are an integral part. You will also learn much more about your role in the grand design of the future. You are embarking on

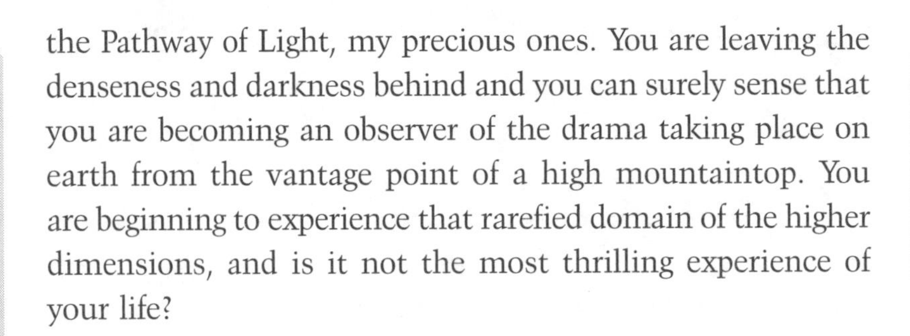

the Pathway of Light, my precious ones. You are leaving the denseness and darkness behind and you can surely sense that you are becoming an observer of the drama taking place on earth from the vantage point of a high mountaintop. You are beginning to experience that rarefied domain of the higher dimensions, and is it not the most thrilling experience of your life?

You who have worked, meditated, studied, loved and dedicated yourselves to this pathway of Light for so many years now are finally beginning to realize just how vast and all-encompassing this process is. You are beginning to ask about your slumbering brothers and sisters, "Why can't they see? Why can't they feel the wonder, the joy and the love?" They will, dear ones, they will. That is the task before you now: to spread your excitement and joy, to shout from the roof tops the miracles that are manifesting for you every day, to share your insight, your compassion, your wisdom, your knowledge. It is wondrous to observe the synergy that is building: a group initiates an event somewhere and suddenly it is picked up around the world by other groups until there is a wave of energy surging forth, connecting, vivifying and transforming humanity to another level of awareness.

Gateways, or Stargates as you like to call them, are being opened or expanded at a greatly accelerated rate, enabling us to interact more completely and powerfully with humanity. And time is of the essence, dear and faithful ones; the greater the number of awakened souls, the easier the transition will be when the momentous changes that are being foretold occur.

And so you see, my beloved friends, you are in the midst of a grand, miraculous event. It is imperative that you stay

firmly anchored in your body, while you also diligently work at completing the integration and merging of your soul into the new energy center between the heart and throat area, thereby igniting the process of building your etheric Light body. Many of you have completed this integration and are moving into even higher initiations on the way to merging with vaster fragments of the greatness of who you are.

Continue to join together, dear ones, in meditation and prayer—supporting, teaching and learning together. It is more important than ever. The event you are all calling the 12:12 will be another giant leap in consciousness, bringing together Light workers in numbers greater than ever before. It will be a wonderful experience if you are able to do so, but you do not have to travel to a sacred area of the earth to participate. You are building your own sacred places of Light. Join together that we may infuse you with a new level of truth and awareness; raise your voices in celebration, dedication and thanksgiving, and I promise that I and the entire Spiritual Hierarchy will join with you, as well as all of our beloved galactic friends. We are well on our way to being reunited and we will, together, infuse this galaxy and eventually this particular universe with the Light of the magnificent Creator of All. I AM Archangel Michael and I bring you these truths.

34. The Why of Me

Along the way I stop to see

If I can find the why of me;

The "who am I" that's deep inside,

The real me that tries to hide.

But out I peek so you can glimpse,

Now and again, just by chance,

The curtain slips, defenses down,

And for a moment, there I am.

The who, the how, the why of me,

To all but God, a mystery.

Ronna Herman

35. Archangel Michael's Message on 12:12

Beloved Masters of Light, I bring you greetings from the Most High. You have had memories and whisperings, myths have been brought down from many centuries past of the great Golden Ages that humanity experienced on earth long, long ago. You have heard, you have dreamed and wished that there was truth in the predictions foretelling of another great golden age, a thousand years of peace and wonder. Well, dear and precious ones, we wish to tell you they are true and that time is fast approaching.

Twelve is a very important number in your galaxy. In your Bible, the number twelve is mentioned over a hundred and fifty times—the twelve apostles, the twelve disciples of the Buddha, the twelve tribes—on and on. You have twelve signs and twelve houses of experience in your zodiac, twelve hours on your clock to separate day from night, and twelve months in your year to mark the passage of time.

When your planet sank down into density and limitation, deep into the third-dimensional experience, you were cut off from the magnificence of the life-giving energies of the twelve rays, the twelve chakras, and disconnected from the twelve strands of DNA. A quarantine or barrier was placed around your planet for, you see, the resonance of negativity and the disharmonious energies that spewed out into the astral planes were not to be allowed to infect or affect the rest of your solar system and your galaxy. But that time is past, dear ones, and through the efforts of wonderful beings like you who have walked in faith, who have struggled through all the many trials, who have begun to be daring and bold enough to access the Light and anchor the Light, to once again feel the desire to come into harmony and unity with the Creator,

you have become transformers, lightning bolts, lightning rods you might say—transducers of energy. You have brought the energy in from the higher dimensions and you have anchored it and, through your unified efforts, you have spread it around your earth.

We have said before that it was not known until this mid-century whether you would, once again, have to experience cataclysm and mass destruction of your earth and humanity, but that is no longer a part of your future.

The number twelve is symbolic of the transition from the physical back to the spiritual and you along with your earth are reclaiming your spiritual heritage. For thousands of years you have resonated to the diminished harmonics of seven: seven chakras, seven Rays and the confines of seven dimensions and sub-planes. You could only access your soul through a thin silver cord of energy and could not experience directly the dynamics and life-giving energy of the five higher Rays of your galaxy and the infusion of golden energy directly from the Source. As you begin to tap into these higher Rays, these powerful, transforming frequencies, and start to bring down and incorporate these more refined energies into your body, they will begin to cleanse and change your cellular structure, to enliven your glands, to ignite the knowledge you have trapped in your DNA and brain cells. This is what will help you integrate and build your Light body, which in turn moves you toward your masterhood and the reality of ascension. You think that you are doing it alone, dear ones, but you are not. You have magnificent and wondrous beings who are helping you, who are here to serve you and assure your success. You see, this is a very precious and special planet, this jewel called earth. It is a planet designed with a great richness of detail, variety and expression from

many star systems and ancient civilizations. And you are Starseeds from many civilizations who were sent as representatives of your race with special encodings to be a part of this bold venture. You came as co-creators, and eventually came into the physical body so that you could experience firsthand what you had created. You were designed to experience emotions, the mental body, the full gambit of the desire body; you were to balance spirit in a physical body and co-create paradise, heaven on earth, as extensions of the God/Goddess/Creator of All, but the greatest gift of all: you were given free will.

As you know, down through the ages, your desires led you in another direction, away from the will of the Creator and you began to feel guilt, fear and limitation. Soon you began to believe the illusion that your physical body and the material world of sight and sound were all there was, that there might possibly be some god out there somewhere, but so far away as to be untouchable, unattainable and that you were not worthy of interacting with the angelic realm or the Creator.

You got caught up in the desire body of emotions and sensation and the ego insidiously took control of your thought processes and your reality. The ego was meant to be the servant of the soul while in the physical body. Now the ego is very important because it was meant to help create your personality as you gained experience. It helps define who you are in the physical. It was supposed to monitor your physical vehicle, to help it function, to notify your soul when it was in distress or danger, but it was to be the servant of the soul, not the director. And this is where many of your struggles have come in, in trying to take back the power you gave your ego and bring it back into proper balance under

the control of your Higher Self. And we want you to know that many of you are doing very well, while the masses still struggle under the dominance of the ego-self.

Now you are to a point in your cleansing, your clearing, in raising your frequencies, your vibratory rate, so that many of you are moving through what we call the spiritual initiations. As you let go of those things which no longer serve you and come into balance in your four lower bodies, you move up the ladder of awareness, into higher wisdom and greater enlightenment. This is what ascension is all about. One day at a time, one step at a time, you are either increasing your frequency or decreasing your frequency; you are either ascending or you are descending. It is no longer a valid option to coast or drift; you must make a choice, and the time is now.

Many of you are now radiating enough love, enough Light, enough beauty that you have, or will, come under the direction, into the notice of one of the Masters. You have become what is called a disciple on the path. Now if you do not already feel a great affinity toward or resonate to the energy of a particular Master, put out the call; ask to be told. The answer may come to you in a dream, or there may be a message or mention from that beautiful being in every book you open, and it will stir your soul. Someway they will come into your mind and will come to your notice. These Christed-beings, these Ascended Masters have walked the earth and have experienced all of life's trials and tribulations, just as you have, and so they know what you are feeling and the challenges you must face. They are very compassionate, very loving, and they will begin to overlight you with their attributes; they will begin to give you all of their vast wisdom, love and strength, along with the benefit of their experience.

You do not have to do it alone. Allow us to help you, allow us to smooth the way.

Now this great ascension gateway, this highway of Light that is opening, has been planned since the inception of this great experiment on earth. You volunteered for this mission and have been brave and dedicated to your purpose even after you forgot and fell under the spell of illusion. You were not meant to struggle forever without assistance and there has always been a master plan for your rescue or retrieval.

See in your mind's eye this magnificent gateway and see a very narrow path leading through that gate—yes, it is rather steep, but it is not insurmountable. Off to the side, there are several other paths; they are on a more gentle slope, a little easier to traverse, but eventually, after they make a detour, they merge back into the main pathway, and they too will go through the gateway. It is your decision as to whether you go directly along this narrow and wondrous pathway into your higher consciousness, into your divinity, claiming your birthright, or take the detour and, later, follow those brave ones who surge forth, clearing the way, regardless of the cost. It may seem frightening and it may seem arduous, but we tell you that no matter what difficulty you might experience, the gifts you will be given outweigh them far and beyond. You are so close—step through beloved ones—trust us, step through.

Believe us when we say that the initiation you take tonight is even more important then the ones you have experienced in ages past, in many lifetimes. In Egypt when many of you lay in the sarcophagus and faced the terrors of your ego and soul, some of you did not make it; no, many of you did not make it. Some of you transcended, and had to start

over. But it is time to let go of those fears, dear ones. You no longer have to experience the difficult and rigid rules and trials of the past in order to move through the initiation process. You have been given a dispensation, the gift of grace, to assist you along the way so that you may move quickly through the process, but you must make the commitment and dedicate yourself in body, mind and spirit in order to take advantage of this great window of opportunity.

And now allow us to give you another gift, if we may. Close your eyes and settle into the sacred chamber of your heart center. See it begin to glow with the fire of a blazing golden Sun and see yourself in this chamber as a beautiful diamond, or a crystal, or perhaps a star. How do you imagine your perfect Light body? What will it be like, do you remember? You can make it a human form if you wish, but feel it—feel how light it is, feel how vibrant, how free, without the confines and restrictions of the physical structure. Now feel yourself begin to drift up and out your crown chakra; you are floating, drifting so freely and so wondrously, out into the higher dimensions, into the sweet, rarefied air of the more refined frequencies. You are resonating, vibrating—so aware—you feel so alive and then, off in the distance, you see a magnificent crystal cathedral. There are two great, arched doors swung wide, and there is a golden beam of light that catches you up and lifts you and brings you to the entrance of this doorway. As you step inside, you look around and you see many, many faces that you recognize. This great room is filled with the most wondrous and beautiful beings. The music is so sweet it brings tears to your eyes and the radiation of loving energy is almost overwhelming. You are caught up in the crowd as you walk down the aisle. You cannot see what is ahead for a while until, suddenly, those in

front of you go to the right and to the left and you are left standing before a magnificently dressed man who radiates power and yet, great compassion, and beside him is an elegant, stately lady in shimmering garments, emitting an aura of love and benevolence. The most gloriously beautiful pair you have ever seen. They are radiant and look down on you in recognition and with great love, and your heart overflows with gratitude. They are representatives of the Almighty God and Goddess, Creators of all, and if their energy were not stepped down, you know that you would not be able to look upon them or stand in their great energy field.

Now this beautiful female, this lovely lady, steps forth and asks you to open your hand. She taps the palm of your hand with her scepter and there appears a sparkling, iridescent pink stone, and then the magnificent, compassionate, wondrous man steps down and he too touches your palm and a blazing blue light pours forth from his scepter. The blue and pink lights merge and the stone turns into violet, into a bit of Violet Flame. You clutch this beautiful stone to your heart and you know that this is a gift of the essence of the God and Goddess. After one last look of adoration, you turn and walk down the steps, back down the aisle and out the door. You step onto the beam of light that brings you back, back down into your crown chakra and, once again, you settle into your heart center.

Know, dear ones, we have infused the small purple stone that you were given this night with the essence of the Creator, with the Violet Transmuting Flame, a wondrous gift in remembrance of this auspicious occasion.

Begin to use the five higher Rays that are now accessible to you; bring them into your life. They are available to assist

you, to bring you joy and great benefit and help speed you along the path of ascension. Expect miracles, beloved ones, for there are wondrous miracles waiting for you to claim them. You are to be the new world servers; you are the vanguard, you are the Wayshowers, you are the ones who will be called to go out and herald the Golden Age of tomorrow.

The more you use the gifts given to you, no matter how small or insignificant you think they are, the more will be given. You are beautiful and magnificent beings and we are honored to serve you.

I AM Archangel Michael and I bring you these truths.

36. It Is Time to End the Illusion of Separation

Beloved Masters of Light, as you don your new cloak of awareness in preparation for your existence in the higher dimensions, we would like to give you some ideas to see if they fit with your emerging picture of reality.

Let us delve into the illusion of separation of masculine and feminine energies, your ideas regarding sexuality and what you call "The Battle of the Sexes."

Not only are you bringing into balance your physical, mental and emotional/ego bodies, and the right and left hemispheres of the brain, but you are, after so many ages, in the process of integrating the polarities of masculine and feminine energies.

The battle began when the energies of the God and Goddess were pitted against one other. The Divine Power/Will aspect of the Father was misused, as was the Divine Love/Wisdom aspect of the Mother. This began in the middle era of Atlantis and progressed until, gradually, the Goddess withdrew from the earth, leaving just a fragment of her energy, thereby making way for a patriarchal society and the subjugation of all those in the female bodies.

There was also another time, which is not often spoken of except as myth, the time of the Amazon female society where men were used as slaves and subjected to many of the same inequities and atrocities that females have been forced to bear for the last 10,000 or so years. Not for as long a time, and it did not happen to as many souls, but it is still imprinted on the etheric records of many.

It is time for this battle to come to a close and for each of

you to remember and accept the fact that you have been both male and female in many incarnations. You have been the victim and the victimizer; you have wielded the masculine energy of Power/Will, and you have spread the Love/Wisdom of the feminine aspect. It is time for these energies to merge, modify, unite and strengthen each other until they are totally in balance and harmony in each of you.

There are many beautiful females in embodiment at this time who much prefer being in the masculine body, but they agreed to incarnate in the feminine so that they could be representatives of how an empowered woman is to live, act and function—powerful, action-oriented, outward-focused, using the dynamics of will, but with discernment and compassion, in unison with the Love/Wisdom aspect of the Goddess.

There are also a great number of males who have had many more lifetimes in the feminine body, and are therefore more comfortable in that mode, who agreed to incarnate during this era to be living examples of how a man can still be manly and yet show emotions, be creative, compassionate, nurturing and gentle.

The division between the sexes is narrowing and the rules and regulations that separate them (according to mass consciousness) are becoming less defined. Women are active and successful in the world of commerce and public life and it is becoming accepted for a man to maintain the home and nurture the offspring if he so desires. But you still have a long way to go.

Sexual energies are still a battleground between men and women of earth. The desire body is still very much in control of the psyche of many of you. You are still looking for

that perfect mate to make you feel whole, to fill in or smooth over the areas of pain and loneliness. We tell you, dear ones, it will not work, and yet many of you go from one experience or relationship to another, each ending in disaster and leaving more pain and broken lives in your wake.

The energy of the Goddess is once again returning to earth. Many of you are awakening to the fact that an important part of your mission is to anchor this energy and be a representative of the feminine ray of Love/Wisdom. Many brave men and women have agreed to be examples or pioneers as the new prototype males and females of the future: a perfect balance of masculine and feminine energy, working in harmony, complementing, assisting, and interacting in every aspect of life's experience.

Before you can find that perfect mate, or a divine complement, you must each focus on integrating the polarities of both male and female energies within. Accept your divinity—love who you are as a divine representative of the God/Goddess. Stop warring with your physical body and accept it as the temple of your Spirit and bring it into wholeness with the assistance of your I AM Presence. Stop being a martyr and giving your power away, or being an overbearing aggressor looking for acceptance and recognition. Claim your identity and your uniqueness; stop comparing yourself to anyone else. Use the talents you brought forth in this lifetime to help you move through the remaining obstacles that are keeping you from your mission and the ultimate goal of masterhood.

Stop using your sexual energy as a weapon or an escape. Begin to use it as the empowering, awesome gift it was meant to be. Honor your body and the body you choose to merge with. You take on much more than just bodily fluids when you have sexual interaction with another. You take on the energies in their auric field for better or worse and it can take years for these to dissipate or dissolve in the third-dimensional modality.

Concentrate on yourselves for the present, dear ones, merging with your own soul, bringing into balance your mental and emotional natures. Endeavor to develop your creative abilities, reactivate those hidden talents and gifts that have lain dormant for so very long. Then you will emerge as a dynamic being of wholeness, ready to share that wholeness with another, if you so desire. And, as a reflection of your empowered self, you will choose another being who will add to and complement who you are, not detract. Through the synergy and dynamics of the two, you can create even greater miracles.

You are being brought together, reunited with your soul family and the many facets of yourself; the illusion of separation is beginning to melt away and will, in the coming years, completely disappear. Placing your hopes, dreams and aspirations on another person, no matter how wonderful or perfect he may seem, is negating your own power and potential perfection. You are to acknowledge that you are a master in your own right, no better, no less than another, but equal in the eyes of the Creator.

Accepting the responsibility of who you are is the first step. Stop blaming your failures or weaknesses on another person, male or female, or the establishment, is the next step. Merge and acknowledge your feminine and your masculine attributes and use them to create a beautiful, totally balanced, self-contained, spiritual being in a physical body. Then and

only then will you step forward into the role you accepted before this incarnation, that of an integrated, loving, empowered extension of the God/Goddess/Creator.

We of the higher realms are what you call androgenous, unisexed, a combination of masculine and feminine attributes. We do, however, express all the myriad facets of each, and yes, we too have our preferences, however these are never at odds or out of balance and harmony. We use them as expressions of energy to accomplish the task at hand, at times, using the energies of the Father, forcefully, actively, dynamically, and at other times, using the creative attributes of the Mother, sending waves of love, wisdom and compassion.

It is time, dear ones, time to end the separation. Integrate and harmonize, once and for all, the polarities within you, and then come join us. We have many new adventures to experience, new worlds to create. I AM Archangel Michael.

37. Celebrate the New Beginning

Beloved Masters of Light, as you focus on the days of celebration and come to the end of your year, we would have you pause a moment to examine what has transpired—how you have grown, how your perception has changed and how the world around you has evolved. Many of the changes are subtle and those who are unaware can only see that there seems to be more chaos and destruction, but we know that great changes have been wrought and humanity is moving toward a whole new experience.

Many of you celebrate the birth of the Christ child in the month of December, although this event has taken on a somewhat different connotation and has lost much of its beauty and solemnity, resulting in a frenzy of gift-buying and gift-giving. We suggest that you give yourselves a more precious gift and begin to see these holi-days and sacred days in different ways. What happened 2000 years ago was indeed a miraculous event and a great Avatar was born to show humanity the way back into the Light of the Creator. Now it is time to celebrate the return of the Christ energy or Christ-consciousness, and that birth will take place within the soul of each of you when the time is right. The beloved Jesus came to show the way, just as other great Avatars have, and it is time that you accepted the gift that has been offered you, a gift far more precious than you can purchase in one of your department or jewelry stores.

The second coming of Christ, as it has been heralded, is now in progress as each of you make a sacred place in your heart and reunite with your Soul Self, which paves the way for the Christ-consciousness to overlight and work through you. This is the true meaning of the prophesied Second Coming,

and is not just a gift for those who embrace Christianity, my beloved friends. The meaning of Christ and the Christ energy is that perfect, divine infusion from the Creator, the divine heritage of all humanity, yea, all beings in existence throughout all Creation. Buddha carried this energy, as did Rama, Mohammed, Krishna and many others. You carry a Spark of this Divine energy as well. Please accept the wondrous truth that you ALL are brothers and sisters—you all originated from the ONE SOURCE and to that SOURCE you will return.

The cosmic event you called 12:12 was an opportunity for you to rededicate and reaffirm your commitment to Spirit and your divine destiny, a promise you made many ages ago before incarnating in the physical body on your earth. Many who made that commitment have not awakened sufficiently to answer the call of their Higher Self, and many others have fallen by the wayside because they did not have the strength or dedication to overcome the trials and obstacles along the way. But the good news is that many, many of you have stayed true to your promise and dedicated to your mission, and therefore, this conscious recommitment was an important step for you.

We understand that you feel as if you have been in a whirlwind this past year, but we tell you this, precious ones: the next two years of your time are going to be even more dramatic, more awesome, and more unpredictable. Many of you are ready to work under the guidance of one of the Ascended Masters. If you do not already resonate to a particular one of these wonderful beings, they will make themselves known to you by various means. As you come under their guardianship, they will begin to overlight you with their wisdom, strengths and abilities, thereby facilitating the integration of

the five higher rays and the higher chakras into your four lower bodies.

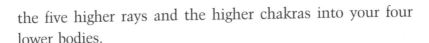

You are to be the new world servers, you see, the physical extensions of the Spiritual Hierarchy. This is what you have been preparing for and why it is so critical that you bring yourselves into harmony and balance in the physical arena.

As the masses begin to awaken and pay heed to their soul's nudgings, they will need guidance, gentle nurturing and support. They will be seeking answers and there is not time for them to wade through all the mass of information that has been brought forth in the last thirty or so years. They will need living examples and simple explanations and that is where you, the vanguard of the New Age come in.

Many of you are ready to be shown exactly what your mission, your area of expertise, will be—many of you already know, but will have new gifts of awareness given you to assist you in your work of the future. You have moved through a gateway, dear ones, the gateway that leads to the future. The time of preparation is over, and now the grand event begins.

During these final years of your century, it is of vast importance that you defuse the fear and negativity wrought by those who preach of doom, gloom and destruction. The end of the world is not upon you, but the ending of an era and the beginning of a bold New Age, a bright future filled with promise. Do not resist; allow the changes to unfold, creating a new reality, a firm foundation for your expanded awareness. As you are transformed and begin to function in your new enlightened state, others will take heart and dare to investigate and test the information you present to them. This is when the rippling effect will begin among humanity as a whole. You will be living, tangible proof of what you teach.

No longer will they be able to deny the emerging wisdom and the new truths you represent.

There will be some friction and resistance from the old guard: religious, social, political, etc., but do not be distracted, dear ones; stay true to your vision and purpose. Walk gently, but boldly; use discernment, but do not deviate from your truth and integrity. We walk beside you, and you are being infused with greater and greater surges of Love/Wisdom from the Creator of All. How can you fail? I, Archangel Michael, bring you these truths.

38. My Search

Why search I in times of quiet?

What makes you smile, or your eyes alight?

Across your mind what shadows fall,

What sad thoughts do you recall?

What makes your spirit withdraw from mine,

Leaving me alone, suspended in time?

To blend with you my Essence seeks,

Two lonely halves, a whole to make.

Ronna Herman

39. It Is Time to Initiate a Soul and Bodily Cleansing

Beloved children of Light, I, Archangel Michael, bring you greetings in this the beginning of your new year, 1995. I would like to propose to you that you initiate a process, a soul and bodily cleansing, if you will.

Many of you periodically initiate a physical housecleaning process, a detoxification or revitalization of your internal organs. This is most desirable and will be of great benefit for you in your emotional and mental cleansing process as well. How can you fill your being with pure light energy when you are filled with toxins and impacted poisons accumulated over the years?

It does not have to be anything drastic: an intestinal cleanse is desirable, or a week of eating light, live foods, such as fruits, vegetables, juices and plenty of pure water. Give your digestive system a rest, dear ones. Allow it to regain its resilience and strength, so that it will function at maximum efficiency. There are many programs available, so please avail yourself of the one you feel will be the most beneficial to you. Do not be afraid of failure. Ask your Spirit Self to guide you to the right process and then ask for the strength and will of Spirit to assist you through the process.

The rewards will be multifaceted. First, your health and physical well-being will greatly improve and you will be laying the groundwork for the next part of the process: preparing yourself for an emotional and mental housecleaning in order to accomplish a closer partnership and communication with your Spirit.

These coming years will be miraculous times, dear ones, but you must be prepared to receive and take advantage of what is being offered to you. A car filled with dirty oil or with a sluggish engine does not function better just because it is washed and shined or because fuel is added. It must be cleaned and tuned and brought into harmony with its many parts or it will not operate efficiently. Your physical being is no different.

Are you ready to receive the miracles in store? It is up to you, dear ones. You can wish, ask, desire or dream all you want, but if you do not take the steps necessary, or if you send wrong or conflicting signals to Spirit, be assured, you will not attain the desired results.

We ask you to begin an ongoing conversation with yourself, asking pertinent questions that pertain to your life's path or spiritual growth. Concentrate on one question at a time, and then ask that the answer be given you. Go forward in anticipation, knowing that the answer will be forthcoming. Listen carefully to what others say to you, or what you are led to read. The answer can come from any source—a dream, a book or a conversation, but you must be watchful and attentive. And then if the information resonates with your inner truth, you must heed the answer and follow the guidance given to you.

Every day expect the unexpected. Know that there are great and wondrous changes in store; like a child, live in anticipation of your highest good. Tap into your thought processes, monitor them and determine if they are negative or positive thought-forms, for this is what is building your future. Arise each morning affirming that you will make the most of that day. Call upon your I AM Presence to give you wisdom, discernment and direction and place yourself in an aura of love and peace.

See what a great difference it will make. Are you brave

enough to surrender your future to Spirit, to allow it to unfold in its perfectness? All obstacles or challenges placed before you are for your growth. Once you accept them as such and seize the opportunity to gain knowledge and awareness, they will no longer seem like obstacles.

Dear ones, spend a few moments every day and focus on your heart center, envision the love of your Christ-consciousness pouring down upon you and en-lighten-ing your spinal column like a fluorescent tube. Feel this energy permeate your body and then concentrate on sending the surplus out your solar plexus in a stream of Violet Light or as a Violet Flame. If you would do this every day, the miracles you would bring forth for yourself, that you would help create for others and the world, are without measure.

It is time for you to begin to be co-creators of heaven on earth. The time of being a novice and a student are quickly coming to a close. It is time for you to claim your masterhood, and assume the full mantle of responsibility that you consented to so long ago. It is not the time for the faint of heart, or for vacillation. It is the time of action, fruition and culmination. What your part in the process and what your share of the riches of Spirit will be is all up to you, dear ones. Please begin. Begin now, where you are with what you have. Guidance and direction will be forthcoming with every positive step you take. This we assure you.

WE TELL YOU IT IS THE TIME OF MIRACLES, DEAR ONES. WILL YOUR CUP RUNNETH OVER, OR WILL YOU BE LEFT EMPTY HANDED? The decision is up to you.

We have the utmost faith in you, and are waiting to answer your call, every moment of the night or day. I, Archangel Michael, bring you these truths.

40. The Gateway to the Golden Age Is Open—The Ascension Drama Begins

Beloved Masters of Light, many of you are feeling a myriad of sensations and emotions since the profound experience of the opening of the 12:12 Ascension Gateway. You cannot move through an initiation into a higher frequency, or experience the removal of old impacted energies, without an outward manifestation of either joy or bliss, or perhaps feeling somewhat off balance, no longer having a sense of structure or, possibly, feeling somewhat vulnerable. As you remove those energies from your body and auric field, let us call them dark crystals for the lack of a better term, it leaves a void, even a sense of loss. After all, dear ones, you have lived with and been influenced by these negative energies for many ages and although they did not function from the standpoint of power, love and unity, nevertheless, it is what you are accustomed to and what you have been conditioned to believe is your true sense of self.

We ask you to bear with the process of transformation; it will become easier as you progress. Envision these impacted energies being lifted from deep within your cellular structure and moving out of your physical body. As they move through your etheric web, envision them as magnets drawing out the dark, impacted masses of negative energy that are stuck like glue to this web that encases your physical body. Now see them moving out farther into your emotional body and gathering all the misqualified energies within this energy field: feelings of unworthiness, fear, anger, stress, anxiety, etc., all those energies that are keeping you off balance and in pain. As these crystals move out farther, they move through the mental body and draw forth all your rigid thoughts, judgments, ego-dominant impulses which keep you

disconnected from Spirit. After you sense that you have released as much as you are ready to release for the present time, see these energies move out from your mental body and ask your I AM Presence to send down a great shaft of Light and lift these dark crystals up to be requalified into pure Light substance.

Now, sense magnificent, powerfully energized Light Crystals of every hue and shade, especially the colors of the five new Rays being pulsed down in waves from your I AM Presence and filling all the areas left vacant by the removal of these dark crystals. This will build your light quotient very quickly and facilitate the manifestation of your wonderful Light body in preparation for ascension.

The era of preparation and planning was completed with the opening of the 12:12 Gateway to Freedom. The grand drama is about to begin and the players are in place—those of you bold enough to step forward and claim your role by recommitting to the call of your highest destiny for this New Age. Make no mistake, it was a time of initiation; however, you did not have to be with a large gathering or at some sacred site to participate. Many of you quietly affirmed your dedication in solitude or with a few close friends, and yes, some of you who are still a little meek and unsure of your worthiness stepped through this portal and took the initiation during your sleep time. Your Higher Self is not about to let you off the hook just because you have a few doubts and still carry the burden of some imbalanced fragments. There is still time to clear and balance these energies and the sooner and more thoroughly you do this, the easier the times ahead will be. You see, dear and precious ones, the ascension process is now in full swing and the power is building. Masses upon masses of negative thought-forms are being swept from

the consciousness of humanity. The Light is infiltrating into places that have been hidden in darkness for ages past, and those in power and authority who are still steeped in the third-dimensional mentality will see their empires crumble away.

Expect some growing pains, expect some discomfort, but allow your Spirit to shield you and ease the way. We have told you that there are miracles forthcoming and the excitement is building as wondrous gifts and great assistance are given to more and more of you. You have earned the rewards you will be reaping—you have affirmed and believed and now you will see what your faith and dedication can manifest in your personal life and eventually in the world.

Many of you are quickly moving into a higher awareness. Even that which seemed so important last year now seems to have lost meaning and validity. As you release old relationships, jobs and habits that no long serve you, a number of you will be led, almost miraculously, to reconnect with members of your Light family. Many of you will feel the urge to migrate to new areas, not out of fear, but out of a feeling of anticipation and excitement. You will be drawn away from the large cities and into sparsely populated, pristine areas. Here, in these remote, untouched lands, much energy will be focused and the various frequencies of these places will call to you. You will feel at peace and as if, at last, you are home. Here will be built the new prototype communities of the coming New Age. Here you will add the vibrations and harmonics of your soul, and others of like vibration will be drawn there also. You are not the person you were a year ago, and the change in humanity will be even more dramatic in coming years. You see, what took place on 12:12, 1994, was a roll call, you might say. You, and you alone, determined what place in the scheme of ascension would be yours, what

part you would play, how you would serve, if you would serve, or if you would continue to be the victim in the drama of illusion in the third-dimensional reality.

You all are destined to take part in the ascension process, but when, dear ones, when will you choose as your time? The window of opportunity is open wide and the march has begun. The lines are forming, waiting to step on the escalator, on the highway to the stars and a bold new drama that is ready to unfold. What part will you play? We have a most glorious new costume waiting for you, dear ones, a garment of Light, and the role of an Ascended Master awaits you, if you will only reach out and claim it.

We await your decision, beloved ones, only you can choose your destiny. I AM Archangel Michael and I bring you these truths.

41. The Photon Belt— What Is it Really All About?

Many Light workers are asking questions about the predicted coming event: the earth and our solar system moving into the Photon Belt; the possibility of five days of darkness and the total breakdown of all electrical power systems, including batteries. It has been predicted that this event would, in all probability, happen as early as March 1995, or the latest, sometime in 1996. In 1981, it was predicted that there was a good possibility it could happen as early as July 1992.

Everyone wants to know what consequences it will have on them and their families, how it will affect the earth and humanity. We all need to use our own thought processes and seek wisdom and our own truth and validation when we are faced with predictions of coming events that might have a major impact on us and our loved ones. To have a better idea of what a "photon" is, I looked it up in Webster's Dictionary and it states, "A photon is a quantum of electromagnetic energy having both particle and wave properties; it has no charge or mass but possesses momentum and energy." The energy of light, x-rays, gamma rays, etc. is carried by photons.

The following is Lord Michael's view of the Photon Belt's impact and what it means to humanity:

Beloved Masters of Light, as with other predictions of cataclysm, destruction, changes in nature or supposed "Acts of God" that leave humanity feeling helpless and uncertain as to their future, this foretold event strikes fear in the hearts of humanity, one and all. Regardless of the fact that your earth is slowly stifling and dying from the pollution of negative thought-forms and toxicity, regardless of the masses of humanity that live in abject poverty and misery, and the feelings of futility and hopelessness that have crept into the consciousness of all humans, no matter their station or circumstances, it is still the mode of human thought: "The known, no matter how inadequate, is better than the unknown."

Radical change for humanity, whether it agrees or not, whether it cooperates or not, must happen. Those who struggle, kick and scream every step of the way are the ones who feel as though their lives are falling apart and nothing works or functions as it did in the past. And, those of you with the dedication, insight and will who have sought knowledge, Love/Wisdom and expansion, thereby bringing your consciousness into harmony with the new vibrational frequencies, are finding a wonderful flow and synergy in your life's experience.

It is all about evolution, dear ones, moving forward to a new state of being, a state of expanded consciousness. As has been predicted, your earth's rotation has diminished, there has been an internal shift and a straightening of the etheric axis. As has been revealed, there are great pulsations of photon energy (or gamma rays) moving through your solar system for which your scientists have no explanation. You have been feeling the effects or have been under the influence of this new energy since 1962, resulting in the radical changes in weather patterns, more earth movement and volcanic eruptions, etc. The cycles of the universe, your galaxy, your solar system and earth move forward inexorably, with or without your permission and acceptance.

And so, what you wish to know is how and when this will manifest and how it will affect each of you. First of all, predictions are only that, the possibility of a future event happening at a certain time. While your free will does not come into play in this grander event of cosmic order, it will happen whether you agree to it or not; the time frame of when it will happen cannot be predicted with accuracy—we repeat, cannot be predicted with accuracy by anyone, not even the Hierarchy. How it will affect humanity in a broader spectrum can more readily be foretold.

Ponder this, those of you who have worked to raise your vibrations or frequency in body, mind and Spirit have had the frustrating experiences of your electrical appliances going awry, or your car's electrical system functioning erratically, and then suddenly they would run perfectly again, or if you sought to have them repaired, you were told that there was nothing wrong with them. What explains this phenomenon? One and all, they were affected by the increase in your electromagnetic force field. Many of you have already figured out this unusual phenomenon and have endeavored to harmonize your electrical appliances and motor vehicles to your higher frequencies, or have simply waited for them to return to normal. Does this give you a clue?

Without going into the complicated, technical details of this coming event, we will tell you that you are moving into a new space/time continuum. The Omniverse is made up of electricity, electromagnetic energy pulsations; you are electromagnetic energy force fields as well. The approach of this cosmic cloud of energy has been gradual and will continue in this manner so that there will be time for the transition to take place. This is not to say that there will not be radical changes and more erratic events taking place as all humanity and the earth make adjustments to these new frequencies and a new reality. When this space/time overlap is

completed, your earth will move from a third- or fourth-dimensional frequency to a fifth-dimensional frequency. Have we not told you that you were moving toward the fifth dimension? Is this such a surprise?

And so, what is your fear based on—the unknown, being in darkness for a few days, if this is to be the case? There is another scenario predicted, you know? "If the earth enters the Photon Belt first, the sky will appear to be on fire; however, it will be cold light, with no heat." The alternative prediction states, "If the Sun enters first, there will be immediate darkness for approximately 110 hours and there will be panic and chaos."

Well, dear ones, here is where your free will does come into play. Must humanity have this radical jolt of the reality of coming cosmic changes, or will you lift your consciousness enough to make this transition with the minimum of discomfort and pain?

Is this not a symbolic scenario: the sky filled with fiery light and falling stars, with an emergence into Light and new birth of consciousness and a totally different system of harmonics, or total darkness and the complete breakdown of your mechanized society as you know it, at least temporarily, shocking humanity awake?

Just as some of the cataclysmic events foretold for the destruction of much of your land mass have been averted by the dedication of the many wonderful Light workers and, make no mistake, you have made a difference, so can this coming event be one of joy and anticipation. Are you going to fall back into the old mode of fear and feelings of helplessness, or are you going to accept your sovereignty and your masterhood in this coming event as well? Spread the word,

squelch the rumors, tell all who ask that the future is bright with promise for those who will strive for illumination, wisdom, harmony and unity of purpose.

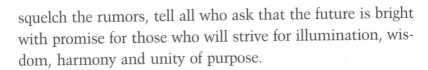

Regardless of the coming events, however they manifest, many of you are aware that you rely too much on the mechanized world and its convenience and comforts. Many of you are feeling the desire and strong impulse to become more self-sufficient, returning to a more natural mode of living, closer and more in harmony with your mother earth and away from the concrete and cacophony of the large cities and all the misery created there. And so, we will tell you that those of you who begin to rely more on Spirit and your own resources and stop depending on your government and large corporations or more "gadgets" to make your life seemingly better, will be the winners in these coming times of transition.

Do not fear the future, dear ones; you are coming into an Age of Light, a golden time of glorious awareness. Is it not worth the slight discomforts along the way?

You are making grand progress, dear and precious ones. Gird yourselves in your spiritual armor and seek the wisdom and illumination that is being offered you. You will not fail if you stay true to your mission. The Angels of Heaven and the Spiritual Hierarchy are with you every step of the way. I AM Archangel Michael.

42. We Offer Encouragement and Loving Assurance for the Changing Times Ahead

Beloved Masters of Light, feel the truth of what I say as it resonates in your heart center and sends out a vibration of love and hope throughout your being. I speak to each of you and I ask you to take heed because of the critical nature of the times to come, because of the vast amount of conflicting emotions you will be experiencing, and the whirlwind of events that will be transpiring in your personal reality as well as your world. I come to give you assurance that from the perspective of the higher realms, the cosmic order of events is proceeding within the proper time frame and we rejoice at the quickening of Spirit in humankind.

This is not the time for the faint of heart or the weak in Spirit. This is the time, after the rededication of purpose and reaffirmation of your mission, for clarity and focus—clarity, dear ones, clarity of action, clarity of mind and heart. We stress this strongly, and remind you that it is of utmost importance at this time, for you are setting the stage for the blastoff into the dimensions of new reality.

More than ever before, we admonish you to guard your thoughts and control your emotions, to carefully monitor the events you set in motion in your life and the effect you have on those around you. Vacillation, doubt, fear or negativity only restrict you and hold you captive in your old reality. At this time, many of you are not sure what course of action to take; you feel the way has not been made clear and you are hesitant or fearful that you will make a mistake. But I assure you, brave warriors, all you have to do is turn inward, heed your feelings and let your intuition gently point the way. Do not worry that you will be swayed from the truth or duped as you have been in the past. We have not come this far and this close to victory to allow you to fall by the wayside or complete the journey unattended. Each of you, in addition to being reconnected to your Soul Self, is surrounded by loving assistants, assigned to you only. You have earned the right to guardianship by your dedication and right action and, henceforth, will travel in the company of the Angelic Host, not just your personal guides or guardians.

Begin now, this moment, to live each day as if it were your last day in the physical. Begin to release all the old baggage of your third-dimensional world, whether it be possessions, relationships, outmoded ideas or philosophies, emotional or mental restrictions, so you will be a clean, clear, receptive channel for the infusion of refined, magnified energy and advanced wisdom that is bombarding your earth.

Make your peace with the world—seek forgiveness and harmonize any and all remaining issues or imbalances that are holding you back. Streamline and redefine your world. No longer participate in activities or duties that are not for the highest and best good of all. You will be amazed at how many people, issues and problems will simply melt away, or fall by the wayside once you commit to your highest purpose.

Become a silent observer, a nonparticipant in the senseless dialogue that is the common mode. Speak with wisdom and discernment so that what you have to say will have significance and impact, and those around you will listen and take heed. Flow gently through your days and nights secure in the knowledge that all is perfect and exactly as it should be. Seek the serenity of your Soul Self and know that nothing but the love of the Creator, through your beloved I AM Presence, can touch you.

There are some of you who are still feeling the effects of residual issues that are in the process of being resolved. I say to you, beloved Masters, gather your cloak of armor, your aura of love and peace about you, and know that the resolution of each situation is at hand. You will not be asked to release or relinquish anything that is not for your highest good and that will not be replaced with gifts, precious beyond measure. It matters not whether it is relationships, possessions, temporary dis-ease, or discomfort of any sort; release them, dear ones, if they are not in harmony with your new awareness. As a master, you will gladly release the old childish, outmoded ways and don the mantle of wisdom and compassion.

This is the time for refining, honing, perfecting the physical vehicle and its environs, as well as strengthening the spiritual awareness within your emotional and mental bodies so that you can begin to experience the new you, the empowered, enlightened Spiritkind you are becoming.

It is also of the utmost importance that you begin to realize that you are an energized, pulsating, vibrational energy source, and as you emit the emotional and mental thoughtforms each moment of your day and night, they have great impact on those around you, your world and most of all upon you. So be diligent, dear ones, of your thought processes, your words and actions. Practice the middle, balanced way and nonjudgment as if your very life depended upon it for, in truth, it does. The swords and barbs of bigotry, judgment, fear and negativity are swift and sure, always hitting their mark and, ultimately, you, as they go full circle.

Both day and night, surround yourself with the golden-white Light of the Christ-consciousness, your magnetic cloak of invincibility, so that not one iota of negativity from any

source can penetrate your force field, thereby creating imbalance and disharmony. See a brilliant shaft of bold, blue Light penetrating your crown chakra and permeating your entire body and then sinking downward to the center of your mother earth. This is my gift to you, the Sword of Right Will, Purpose, Truth and Valor, with the hilt anchored in your heart center, radiating the Love/Wisdom energy of the Goddess.

Go forth each day secure in the knowledge that, once more, you have conquered the world of ignorance, restriction and limitation, that each day brings you closer to that long awaited moment when, once again, the veil of illusion will be lifted and you will see with clarity. You will remember with joy and feel the unity of, and the integration with, that vast loving energy source, your I AM Presence, of which you are an integral part. You will remain separate and apart only within your uniqueness, that which you bring as your gift to the whole, that for which you were sent out to experience many ages past. Fear not that you will lose your individuality, for that is the treasure you were sent forth to seek. This is why we admonish you not to judge yourself by another or any standard of measure. You are one of a kind; you are unique and vital to the whole of Creation and we treasure you for this reason.

And so, beloved ones, as you proceed through this year of great changes and transition, meet each challenge and opportunity head and heart straight on, secure in the knowledge that you are, indeed, on the home stretch: that never again must you walk this way for you are leaving the old world and its rules of restriction and deprivation behind. The Golden Age to come is not just wishful thinking—not just a dream—it is a reality about to be made manifest.

Listen to our words of encouragement in your dreams, feel our loving support course through your veins and, in your times of quiet, listen to the whisper of our voices, for we are calling to you.

Go forth in peace and good cheer, blessed ones; your time is at hand. I, Archangel Michael, always near to guide and protect you, give you these truths to lift and sustain you. THE LOVE OF THE CREATOR AND ALL CREATION ARE WITH YOU. And so it is!

43. The Grand Event Has Begun—Your Success Is Assured

Beloved Masters of Light, do you feel the excitement building, the anticipation increasing, day by day? Do you feel somewhat withdrawn and isolated, as if all those things that seemed so important and were the focus of your attention these past few years no longer have meaning or validity? Do you have trouble concentrating on the mundane chores and details of your everyday tasks or paying attention to conversations? Your reality is shifting and you are experiencing some distortion and, yes, some discomfort as you adjust to the energies of the higher-dimensional frequencies you have begun to access.

Many of you have integrated or balanced many of those external creations that have caused you so much distress. Your relationships are more loving and meaningful. You are beginning to believe that you have the right to abundance and a steady flow of manifested energy in the form of the material possessions necessary for your comfort and everyday existence. Your creativity is beginning to flourish and take on new dimensions and your health is improving. And so why, you say, are you having such disturbing feelings of fear, loss, anger, loneliness, isolation and frustration which seem to well up from deep within?

As you climb the pathway on the lofty spiral of ascension, via the initiation process, the higher you move, the more refined the energies become and the more subtle the tests, or imbalances become. You have sent forth thoughtforms of love, peace and harmony and these are now manifesting in your immediate surroundings, but you still hold residual imperfect memory cells within your body that are being jarred loose by the Light you are accessing and which has permeated your physical, mental and emotional bodies. These memory cells are floating free and if you do not release them totally, they lodge in the areas where you are still most vulnerable: the solar plexus, creating anxiety and old emotional responses; the lower chakras, activating instinctual memories of survival and fear, or masculine and feminine polarity imbalances; and feelings of inadequacy, or mistrust for the feelings of power or sensitivity you thought you had integrated.

Many of you are feeling distress in various parts of your body and are even manifesting symptoms of pain or discomfort in various organs, but your medical doctors can find nothing physically wrong. Is it so surprising, dear ones? Your allopathic diagnostic tools cannot monitor or register what is wrong with you, although it is to your advantage to go through the process of eliminating any physical ailment to ease your mind so that you will begin to look for the real cause.

My beloved friends, you are mutating! You are in the midst of an intense transformational process and it is happening very quickly. Imbalances that have been stamped on your etheric body for ages are being harmonized. Implants and encodings that have kept you imprisoned and functioning at only a fraction of your capabilities are being released or reprogrammed. Therefore, during this time of transition, you are bound to feel a little out of sync, or out of kilter. You have released so much of the illusion and glamour of the third and fourth dimensions which have manifested in your exterior world, but what you may not realize is that it must also affect your interior world and most specifically, your body.

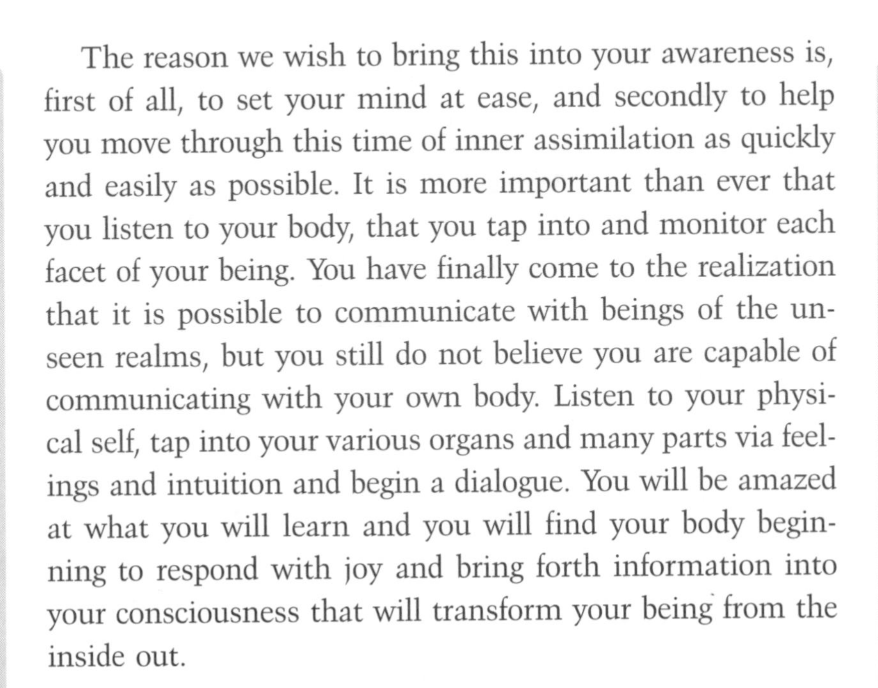

The reason we wish to bring this into your awareness is, first of all, to set your mind at ease, and secondly to help you move through this time of inner assimilation as quickly and easily as possible. It is more important than ever that you listen to your body, that you tap into and monitor each facet of your being. You have finally come to the realization that it is possible to communicate with beings of the unseen realms, but you still do not believe you are capable of communicating with your own body. Listen to your physical self, tap into your various organs and many parts via feelings and intuition and begin a dialogue. You will be amazed at what you will learn and you will find your body beginning to respond with joy and bring forth information into your consciousness that will transform your being from the inside out.

You are not yet comfortable with your new awareness or reality as you slip in and out of the higher-dimensional frequencies. You are ascending, dear ones; you are in the midst of the process. Most of you have left the third dimension behind and have moved through much of the fourth density expression. You are operating from a vantage point of seeing these lower realities through a haze or an almost dream-like state, where you are aware of them, but they no longer affect you or impact your consciousness. You are tapping into the higher frequencies, but you are still not adjusted to them, nor can you truly grasp the realness of what you are experiencing. This is to be expected for there is no definite demarcation or separation point, but a gradual shifting or interpenetration between the dimensions, you see?

Your ego is also adjusting to its new role as the servant to your Higher Self, and it is not relinquishing its hold on you without a struggle. Whereas, previously, it whispered to you

that you must have riches, power, beauty, etc., to be worthy, that you must seek love and validation outside yourself, it is now taking a new tack. As you begin to accept your worthiness and the fact that you are a divine being, a blessed fragment of the Creator, it is whispering to you, "What makes you think you are so great? How can you, such an insignificant person, be a bearer of the mighty Christ-consciousness, or a representative of the Hierarchy, or a Master? What makes you think you are worthy of ascending?" On and on it goes, in hopes of recapturing its prominent place in your consciousness.

Do not blame your poor ego; it is only trying to find its proper place in your new Soul-empowered being. Gently reject the whisperings and negative thoughts, saying what our beloved brother Jesus said when he experienced his many days and nights in the desert of isolation in preparation for his mission and ascension, "Get thee behind me, Satan," which was in reality his ego, for it is only through the ego that the negative thoughts can enter your mind. Love, nurture and honor all the many parts or facets of yourself as you move through this critical transition process.

We suggest to you that you not make any major decisions for the present time, dear ones. You are all in what you might call a holding pattern as you move through this intense initiation process that is now in progress. Many of you are asking where you should go and what you should do. Soon, you will know and you will not have to ask or doubt. You will know exactly what you are to do, or if you are to relocate as the visions of your future are revealed to each of you. Spend these coming months clearing up any residual issues or situations that call for attention. Indeed, it is a very secular process you are going through, a time of seclusion and

introspection. Many of you have pulled back from your group interactions and feel the need for solitude. Honor these impulses for they are valid. Even though the ascension process you are experiencing is a mass event, it is also a very private and personal event.

No one has quite the history that you have. No one has quite the destiny that you have before you, and no one else can complete your mission for you. You are a unique creation—one of a kind.

Follow your heart's nudgings, beloved ones; listen to your Soul Self as never before. Tap into the cosmic telepathic airways so that you will be privy to the wondrous information that is being sent forth. Ancient wisdom of the cosmos and knowledge pertinent to the coming Golden Age is beginning to filter down from the highest source of the universe and your galaxy. It is penetrating and permeating your solar system and your planet and those of you who are able to access these divine frequencies and encodings will receive the earliest benefits.

If you think you have not made much progress, look back at who and where you were just a few short years ago and you will realize the amazing transformation you have already made. And yet, it is only the beginning; you are only a shadow of the beautiful, shining being you will be in the days to come. We know, for we have had a glimpse of your future.

As each day goes by, more and more beautiful souls are awakening from their slumber. You, the vanguard, the Wayshowers, who have cleared the pathways and removed many of the obstacles, have your work clearly laid out before you. Your spiritual brothers and sisters will need guidance, nurturing, healing and instruction. They will not have to

travel the uncharted territory you have trod in faith and hope, for you have anchored the Light, channeled the expanded truths, thereby widening the vision for each soul personality, and bringing forth an awareness of humanity's role as an integral part of the universe.

There is excitement and hope stirring in the etheric body of the earth and in the subconscious mind of humanity, and rightly so, for the time of the grand awakening has begun. We watch your progress with great joy and anticipation, for the wonderful experiment for which the earth was created and for which you volunteered will not be a failure after all. You are a resounding success, beloved ones, and your mission is moving toward completion. I leave you surrounded in the gossamer Love/Light of the God/Goddess/Creator and all their emissaries. I AM Archangel Michael.

44. You Are Moving Into the Power of the Trinity

Beloved Masters of Light, another grand event has just concluded and another milestone reached in what might be called the saga of evolution and ascension. Many of you are not aware of the great and far-reaching changes that are in progress in this universe and particularly on your earth, moment by moment, day by day. You are familiar with the concept of the trinity, although there have been many misconceptions and misinterpretations in the past. You, who are in the vanguard of this transformational process, are experiencing multilevels of the trinity concept. You are merging body, mind and Spirit; you are merging personality/Soul, Higher Self/Oversoul with your I AM Presence; you are merging masculine/feminine/androgenous aspects of yourself; and a merger is taking place within the third, fourth and fifth dimensions: gradually, but nevertheless they are coming together as the higher, more refined frequencies override the lower vibrations—blending, harmonizing, lifting. And most important, you are beginning to access the divine essence of God/Goddess/Creator and anchoring these omnipotent energies on earth.

Just as with the Harmonic Convergence, the 11:11 event and the 12:12 ascension activation, along with numerous other lesser events such as the openings of Stargates or attunement and adjustments, vortex clearings, etc., the Wesak Festival on May 12-15, 1995, which was celebrated around the world, was an event of momentous proportions. Whether or not you physically or consciously participated in this event makes no difference; it will have a profound and lasting effect on each of you. It was another time of moving forward as another frequency change took place within and on your

mother earth, and within each of you, as well. More of the lower astral planes were cleared and sealed and more of the veil was lifted between the higher dimensions, making it possible for the rarefied energies of the higher astral planes to move a little closer (or the seventh heaven, as it is sometimes called), to become more accessible for you.

Those of you who were able to absorb the higher frequency infusions will benefit greatly, although it may take some time to totally integrate these new energies and manifest them in your physical reality. Many who attended the various events may feel as if nothing major or Soul-shaking took place but, be assured, much healing and activation for the earth and yourselves was facilitated. A forward or upward shift was accomplished in a greater or lesser degree for each area of earth and each human being, according to their ability to accommodate the infusion of Christ Light, or the pure essence of the Creator.

Many of you stepped into the ranks of what we choose to call "Novice Ascended Masters." No, there was no great mass lifting of physical bodies into the unseen realms, but there was a wondrous mass lifting of Spirit within those physical beings who have prepared the way by harmonizing and integrating the trinity facets of themselves we mentioned earlier, thereby releasing the bonds of illusion that are keeping many beautiful souls ensnared and anchored in the physical-density reality. You are moving into what could be called the "One-hundredth Master" effect as many brave and dedicated souls step through the shining inner door of ascension, clearing the way for others to follow—as the energy intensifies and the soul quickens in the mass consciousness.

Many of you are still hoping to escape by some miraculous

means; some have even secretly yearned for the predicted cataclysmic events to take place so that you might be rescued or beamed up into the Light ships, thereby relieving you of any active participation or responsibility. Or, you are hoping for all the gifts of manifestation or mastership without the discipline, or labor of loving sacrifice necessary to bring you into balance and harmony, or to a state of harmlessness. If every person stopped radiating any negative energy and projected even one percent positive energy or action, your earth would come into balance and be a paradise.

One beloved soul likened your wish for the powers of manifestation to that of allowing an infant to have access to a switch that could activate a nuclear bomb. We will not allow this to happen again. You do not realize how close you've come to total annihilation of your earth and all its inhabitants. No longer will those operating from greed, fear and self-interest be allowed to determine the destiny of earth's evolution. The power is being removed from all those still operating from a third-dimensional mentality and placed in the hands of the new Spiritual Hierarchy, the emerging Ascended Masters, the evolving leaders of the coming age, those who are attuned to Spirit, who have assimilated the wisdom and compassion of their teachers and I AM Presence and have been given a glimpse of the divine plan for the grand New Age to come.

With initiation into the ranks of the masters comes wondrous gifts, but also great responsibility. We must be sure you are ready for the burden that will be put upon you (even though we will help to smooth the way and lighten your load). Your earth is evolving at a dizzying pace and you must adjust or fall by the wayside. The chasm between realities and frequencies is widening on your planet daily. Many of

you now see the third-dimensional activity from a near-dream state; it has no impact on you and you can clearly see through the illusion. This will continue as you access more of your Light body and integrate more of the magnificence of your I AM Presence, until you view your world in a totally new way.

Dear ones, do not judge yourself by any other person or any standard but your own inner knowing and intuition. You each have an integral part to play in this great dance of ascension. Many of you will be teachers at an entry level as more and more of humanity stir and answer the nudgings of divine discontent from their souls and Spirit. A number of you will find it is your mission to help to ease the discomfort and trauma of the physical body as it makes its metamorphosis into a divine vehicle of Light. Many will help establish the new world government, and design the new communities of the future, as well as teach the magnificent souls being born, some now reaching adolescence or young adulthood. But most important, by far, is that you stay attuned to Spirit each and every moment, walking and functioning in perfect harmony with your own divine blueprint, creating love and joy in every moment, no matter where you are or what you are doing. When you can do this, then the magic power of manifestation will be showered down upon you in full measure.

Those of you who have stepped into the rarefied company of the Masters know who you are, but as an Ascended Master, you are to keep your counsel and your silence. You will walk and speak softly, but you will carry a great aura of serenity, authority and power. You will live in joyful anticipation and no matter what task is given, you will perform it with great enthusiasm.

It is time to express joy, dear ones; many of you take

yourselves so seriously. The Creator loves laughter, joy and spontaneity. Joy is the word of the day—remember it: joyful anticipation; joyous, loving interaction; innocent perception; total commitment to anchoring paradise on earth once more; creating a new mind-set of peaceful, loving co-existence where harmony and abundance can flourish.

Release the need for validation outside yourself—that is the old way. In the past, your reality was mirrored back to you via relationships, events and lessons. Release that mode as it is becoming obsolete. Turn inward as you access your beautiful Soul Self and your Christed Higher Self, and for some of you, your Divine I AM Presence is now becoming a part of your consciousness. Find your own truths via your intuition through your vaster self and through telepathic interaction with the Masters and your teachers. Wondrous galactic and universal beings are now available to those of you who have cleared the way and accept the gifts they offer. The ring-pass-not no longer exists; you have available to you wisdom and power that has been withheld from you for thousands upon thousands of years. Reach out with your mind and heart, dear ones; allow your soul to soar and dare to dream the most perfect world you can possibly imagine. It will only be a dim reflection of the glorious reality which is forming in the higher realms and will soon descend to earth. I AM Archangel Michael.

45. The Time of Preparation Is Over— It Is Now Time for Action!

Beloved Masters of Light, as your year moves past the halfway point, let us examine together what has transpired. Although your weather patterns have been extreme, unpredictable and erratic, the shuddering and quaking of your earth has quieted somewhat. The weather patterns are symptomatic of the maelstrom of emotional energy that is being released by humanity (most dramatically in some areas), caught up on the air currents and magnified in your atmosphere. Governmental bodies around the world are scurrying and scheming to regain control of the masses which only creates more discontent and chaos.

Those still caught in the third-density expression are wondering why they no longer receive joy or satisfaction from the old forms of activity. There is unrest in the workplace, job insecurity and feelings of helplessness; the joy of acquisition, or the triumph of winning a power struggle somehow no longer brings the sense of superiority or fulfillment it once provided. Rules and regulations at all levels are being tested, questioned, and demands made for change or modification. Families are in disarray and at a loss as to how to regain the sense of unity, safety and continuity they once had.

These are the dear ones who are hanging on for dear life to the old illusions that are slipping away, dissolving before their eyes. Their world and all they perceive seems to be worsening day by day, as they struggle to hang on to what little they have and maintain some semblance of order and balance. On the other hand, those of you who are flowing with spirit and have diligently worked to harmonize your physical vehicles with the new frequencies are finding a new sweetness

and peace in your world. True, you still have your trials and tests, but you have a heightened sense of awareness and can process and resolve any discordant events very quickly with a minimum of discomfort and energy.

We have told you that the division between the planes of existence is widening and the realities between the beings of Light walking the earth and the unawakened masses are coming to a point of demarcation, or a definite separation. You and your neighbors may live in two different worlds of experience and yet be divided by only fifty feet or so.

Many of you who have moved through the cleansing and initiation process are being told (via whisperings, impulses or channeled information) that it is time for you to emerge from your seclusion—your sanctuaries—your safe havens. That is the next step, beloved Masters. You now have a clear vision of what is transpiring. You can sense the subtleties of what is happening in the world; you can see behind the smoke screens and detect the fallacies and distortion of truth being blatantly fed to the masses. In other words, you are no longer functioning under the influence or ruled by those in power of the third-dimensional world.

You are now under the protection and rulership of a higher authority. Henceforth, you will operate under the guidance of the Spiritual Hierarchy, the Planetary Logos, Sanat Kumara, and even beyond. Those of you who are ready to assume the mantle of authority are being groomed and prepared to step out among the masses. That is what all these past months of cleansing and testing have been for, to see if you are strong enough to withstand the tide of pressure you will receive from quickening humanity.

Some of you who are so eager to share your new truths

and insight are still somewhat naive in thinking that what you now represent and wish to share will be received eagerly, with no resistance, no resentment. In many instances this is true, but we tell you now that you must be prepared for hate, fear, judgment, resistance and persecution. But if you stand in your center of power, within the protection of your Divine Presence and do not get caught up in the negative energies that will be spewed out toward you, you will prevail and remain untouched. This will be one of the greatest examples of the chasm between you and the lower frequencies, dear ones. What you do not resonate with cannot impact or touch you, you see?

Those of you who do not feel that you are one of those ready to step out as a Wayshower or teacher of the new awareness can also take heed and benefit from this message. Monitor how you handle the small conflicts that you are confronted with each day. No matter how frustrating or hopeless a situation is, it can be improved by a shift in attitude and a call for assistance from your wonderful, loyal guides and teachers.

As your world spirals into the next higher octave, time as you know it is moving faster and faster. You are losing a sense of stability and this is partially due to the acceleration of time. The evolution of humankind is also speeding up and so you are no longer comfortable in or understand your bodies, how they function and how they react to different situations and stimuli. You are more sensitive to substances you never even noticed before and also are feeling sensations that are totally new to you. As we have said time and time again, you are MUTATING.

This brings us to the subject of the little ones—the

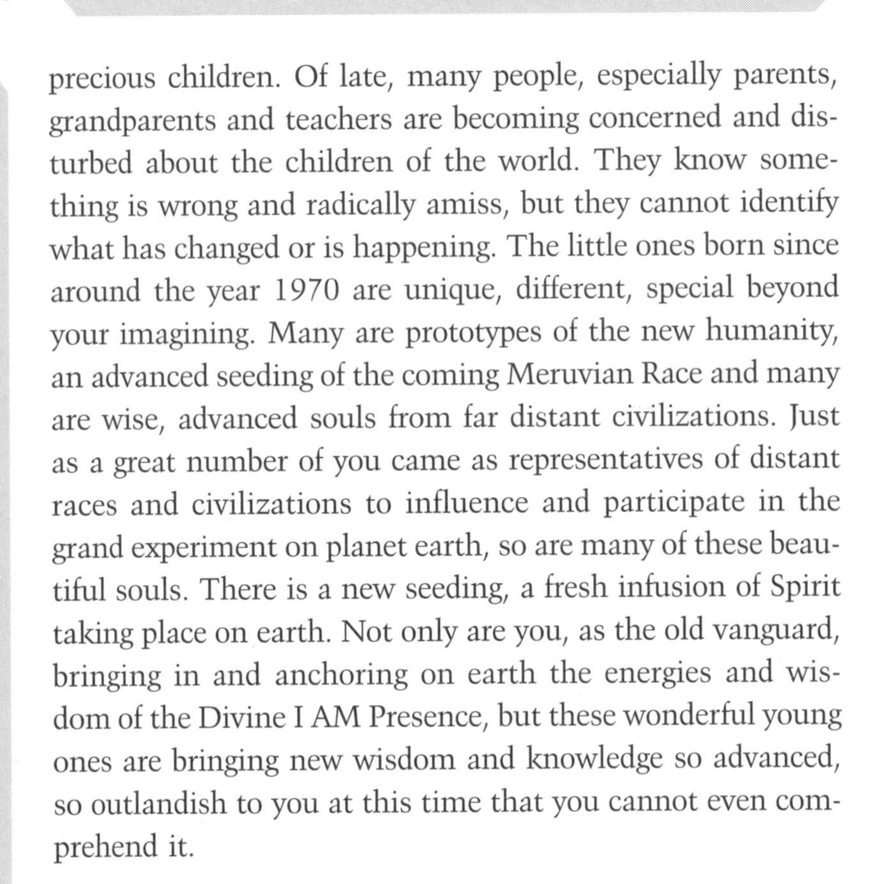

precious children. Of late, many people, especially parents, grandparents and teachers are becoming concerned and disturbed about the children of the world. They know something is wrong and radically amiss, but they cannot identify what has changed or is happening. The little ones born since around the year 1970 are unique, different, special beyond your imagining. Many are prototypes of the new humanity, an advanced seeding of the coming Meruvian Race and many are wise, advanced souls from far distant civilizations. Just as a great number of you came as representatives of distant races and civilizations to influence and participate in the grand experiment on planet earth, so are many of these beautiful souls. There is a new seeding, a fresh infusion of Spirit taking place on earth. Not only are you, as the old vanguard, bringing in and anchoring on earth the energies and wisdom of the Divine I AM Presence, but these wonderful young ones are bringing new wisdom and knowledge so advanced, so outlandish to you at this time that you cannot even comprehend it.

To put this into proper perspective, imagine your world as it was two thousand years ago and how a person brought forward from that time, with the consciousness of that era, would perceive your modern world of today. That is how dramatic the changes will be within the next twenty years of your time.

The children of today require different rules and standards, different care and handling. They are more sensitive, closer to Spirit—the veil between dimensions is thinner and they are bringing with them operative abilities and skills that have lain dormant for thousands of years in most of you, abilities that you have had to work to perfect and refine, attributes that will come naturally to them and will seem normal. Do

not stifle their sensitivities, their creativity, their spiritual awareness. Teach, or just allow them to be the androgenous beings they wish to be: a perfect balance of masculine and feminine energies. Many of these beautiful ones will be ambidextrous, multifaceted in their abilities, talented beyond your imagination if you will only nurture them and allow their spirits to soar. Notice how the heads of many of the babies being born are a little larger than the norm, also slightly elongated as well. Their brains are larger as they were in the days of Lemuria and Atlantis—the mutation process is much more advanced in many of these little ones, you see?

It is time for a complete revamping and restructuring of your educational system. Many of you have been protesting and advocating this for a long time, but time is running out. The schools no longer serve the children, but are constructed to support the bureaucracy and an antiquated system that has completely broken down. There are many extremely qualified Light workers who so desperately want to teach and bring life and truth into the school system, but they are either afraid to challenge the system or have been turned away for being too radical, or nonconformists. This will also be changing, my beloved friends, and soon.

It is not the time for the timid or weak; it is now time to come forth and speak your truth, to take a stand; time to be lovingly assertive, living your spiritual integrity; time to be actively involved. You can make a difference; the tide of ignorance, restriction and limitations can be turned, with waves of love and wisdom as your weapons.

We ask all of you who feel the stirrings of Spirit welling up from within to begin—begin where you are. Use the knowledge and wisdom you have garnered from your own

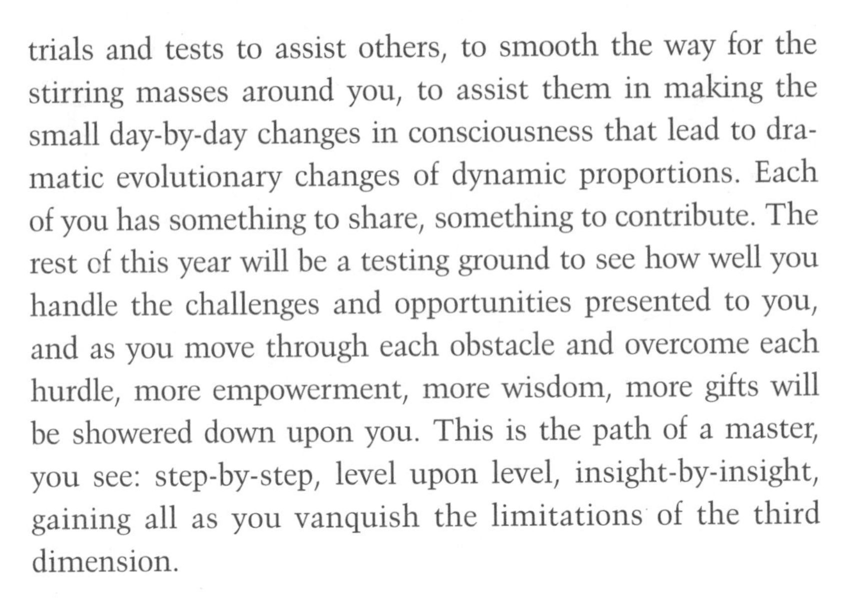

trials and tests to assist others, to smooth the way for the stirring masses around you, to assist them in making the small day-by-day changes in consciousness that lead to dramatic evolutionary changes of dynamic proportions. Each of you has something to share, something to contribute. The rest of this year will be a testing ground to see how well you handle the challenges and opportunities presented to you, and as you move through each obstacle and overcome each hurdle, more empowerment, more wisdom, more gifts will be showered down upon you. This is the path of a master, you see: step-by-step, level upon level, insight-by-insight, gaining all as you vanquish the limitations of the third dimension.

Each day and each step brings you closer to victory. You are making a difference, first with your faith, then by anchoring the Light and surrendering to the Will of the Divine Plan. Now it is time to use the strength and wisdom you have garnered as a Master of co-creation. Many of you have been overlighted by the aura of the Ascended Masters and are physical extensions and representatives of these wondrous beings. Use your powers and abilities with discernment and compassion, dear ones, and hand in hand, united in purpose, we will march forward together to the completion of our mission. I surround you in my aura of loving protection. I AM Archangel Michael.

46. You Are a Divine Representative of the Creator

Beloved Masters of Light, allow me, if you will, to assist you in fine-tuning your new skills and your higher perceptional abilities. It is time for you to function as the master you are becoming, to begin to use your inner senses in addition to your five outer senses. Instead of listening with your conscious mind and physical hearing, begin to feel the resonance of the words that you speak and that are spoken to you. Sense the meaning behind your everyday interaction with others and attune to the vibrational frequencies that are being sent forth. Imagine that you are vision- and hearing-impaired and begin to allow your intuition and extrasensory perception to come to the fore. When you step into someone's auric field, does it feel uplifting and soothing or does it make you want to withdraw from their space? Take stock of your casual and intimate relationships and become aware of those who seem to resonate in harmony with you, and examine your feelings about those who leave you feeling depleted or off balance. You might need to put a loving barrier of Light between yourself and some of those you are out of sync with as you seek to balance and harmonize the energies between you. Also, do not hesitate to send the discordant energy to your I AM Presence to be transmuted and harmonized, along with a request for resolution, "the highest and best good for all." Intent, dear ones, loving soul-focused intent will always lead you to the proper solution.

Each and every encounter and each event you experience during your sojourn along the higher path of awareness has a message for you, very subtle, perhaps, but your Higher Self is presenting different situations and scenarios to you so that you can evaluate or reevaluate your old paradigms, your old

belief structures, and eliminate those that no longer serve you. You are being asked to take a more expanded viewpoint, a broader focus. Practice seeing the panoramic view of your world and interactions instead of concentrating on the "little story" or "little me" syndrome of the third-dimensional experience.

Become a living meditation, whereby you are constantly attuned to the impulses and direction of your Higher Self or your Divine Presence. Imagine this wonderful, vast being (which is who you really are) is perched on your shoulder as you go about your mundane tasks of the day. Would you still act, speak or think as you do now? Begin to get the feeling of "Being in the flow with Spirit." Nothing ruffles your feelings; you handle each situation as it arises with patience and acceptance; you allow no one or no thing to move you out of that blissful center of harmony. This is what it means to function as a master.

You all are aware that as you clear, harmonize and balance your physical, mental, emotional bodies with your spiritual self, you can then begin to access, first your Soul Self, then your Higher Self and, eventually, begin to tap into your Divine I AM Presence. As you clear these frequencies, you begin to access new knowledge and wisdom. Remember who you are, who you have been and how awesome and wondrous the real YOU is. You begin to feel that divine connection with your spiritual family and no longer feel alone...even when in isolation. But are you aware that you are also sending thought-forms, information and new knowledge back along those inner frequencies to your Higher Self and your I AM Presence?

You came to this earth as divine representatives of the

Creator, many of you from ancient, distant civilizations, even other universes, as a part of that stepped-down energy from the God/Goddess/All That Is. Your I AM Presence was given a particular mission, a divine blueprint, as was your Oversoul or Higher Self. And you, as an individual soul fragment or personality of that greater being, were given your particular assignment, or piece of the puzzle to experience and perfect. Now, what is expected of each of you is that, as you gain knowledge and experience, you are to relay that new information back to your Higher Self, which in turn relays it back to your Divine I AM Presence (until you can access that source directly, as many of you are now doing), and this information is sorted, refined and sent on up to the higher levels of creation to be integrated and to modify all the other information that is being gathered from this unique evolutionary experiment on planet earth.

You are allowed to draw from the life-giving force of the Creator in whatever measure you are capable of accessing and absorbing, but there is a Universal Law that you must also contribute or give back some of that Love/Light in devoted service to ALL if you are to continue to grow and thrive spiritually.

It is as if you have been allotted a colored gemstone: uncut, unpolished, unfaceted, encoded with your particular frequency and divine blueprint. Down through the aeons, each experience, whether you are tumbled or tossed about learning life's lessons, thereby smoothing some of the rough edges from your gemstone, or whether you are adding brilliance to this jewel as you fill it with Love/Light, is contributing to the frequency of expression that is uniquely you. It will eventually find its way back to its origins, to harmonize and add its splendor to all the other magnificent, rare jewels, bringing

the wonder and glory of this grand experiment into the consciousness of the Creator of All. Are you aware that you are experiencing the physical reality for all of those great beings, including the Prime Creator, because they are too vast to step their energy and consciousness down to the level of physicality?

What I wish to bring into your consciousness with this scenario is: are your daily actions and thoughts what you would like to have sent up those pathways of Light as your contribution to the Creator? How do you wish to be represented? How would you like to be remembered? Are you sending frequencies of love, compassion, joy and thanksgiving at being a participant in this very important experiment, thereby adding your knowledge and new-gained wisdom to the whole—frequencies that will be worthy of a place in that universal divine blueprint that will be used to create new worlds, new star systems, new civilizations? Or are your thoughts and actions such that they will be turned away as not acceptable to be entered into the cosmic records that are being assembled at this time—records that will tell of the miraculous transformation that has taken place on this small planet called earth...how a small segment of humanity changed the course of cosmic history, prevailing over seemingly insurmountable odds?

Realize, dear ones—believe this, if nothing else; it is true as never before—every thought, deed, action is adding to or detracting from your en-lighten-ment or ascension process, and it affects not only you, but your soul family, your Higher Self and your world. You must realize, once and for all, you are not a separate isolated being, you are not sovereign within yourself. You are a facet of the whole, a cell within the heart of the Creator, and you affect all the rest of creation either

positively or negatively. You wield great power and have a most wondrous opportunity, as never before, to make a difference, to fulfill your divine mission, to be a co-creator of paradise worlds with all the other splendid beings of Light.

Do not let this unusual opportunity pass. It is so simple, beloved friends. First love yourself unconditionally and then extend that same love to all humanity. Practice the gentle, middle way—moderation in all things. Become totally nonjudgmental, allowing each and every individual to find his own truth and follow his own path of destiny. Live in joy, peace and harmony, becoming immune to any discordant energies around you. Envision your own perfect picture of paradise on earth and then follow the nudgings of Spirit which will assist you in bringing your dream to fruition. You have more cosmic energy available to you than ever before. You have more assistance from the higher realms than ever before, but you must do your part by anchoring this energy via your physical vehicle and then, through your own thought processes and actions, bring this vision down from the etheric into the physical expression.

Many of you are evolving so quickly, as you move through the subtle levels of the higher dimensions, you are having a difficult time focusing on your everyday, mundane chores. It is as if you have your feet planted on earth and your consciousness is half in and half out of your physical body. It is very important that you stay grounded and anchored, but for many of you, this will soon change. A number of you are about to take that leap in consciousness whereby you will be able to function simultaneously as a multidimensional spiritual/physical being while still interacting normally in the world. Only those who are gaining this ability will know the difference; however, you will seem more serene, more

efficient, with more vitality, and a greater capacity for love than before.

Many of the Ascended Masters now walking the earth are quiet, unassuming, gentle folk. There are those who are destined to become great speakers and bearers of the new knowledge and wisdom of this time, and those who are destined to perform miracles for the masses, but by and large, most of these beautiful souls will go quietly and serenely about their mission, spreading peace, love and comfort. Where do you stand in this panorama of the shimmering new reality that is emerging on the horizon of your world? Only you can decide.

We offer our wisdom, our love, protection and support, but you must take your dream and bring it to reality. I AM Archangel Michael.

47. I Must Stay

My spirit rests so lightly in my mind

I would like to leave the world behind.

My thoughts soar above and beyond,

While back on earth the pull is strong.

So much to life, it is so sweet,

I must not miss a breath or beat.

The call I feel, the urge is deep,

But there are promises I must keep.

If only I could take you by the heart strings,

And draw you up and away with me,

Up the path to Eternity.

A place of pure white Light and loving energy,

Where my soul yearns and longs to be.

But I cannot go until I know

You all are firmly on your way.

And so for now, I must stay.

Ronna Herman

48. The Archaii (The Feminine Complements of the Archangels)*

Ray	Color	Archangel	Lady	Father Creator Gifts	Mother Creator Gifts
1	Red	Michael	Faith	Divine Will, Truth, Valor	Strengthens faith in yourself: assists you to access and integrate your higher truth while enhancing your courage as you go forth in your endeavor to bring forth the new age of creation.
2	Light Blue	Jophiel	Constance	Illumination	Assists you to manifest and integrate the divine qualities of wisdom, perception and comprehension. Helps understand Universal Laws of Cause and Effect. Brings forth enlightenment needed to turn knowledge into wisdom.
3	Lumin. Pink	Chamuel/ Kamiel	Charity	Divine Love, adoration, spoken word, abstract intellect	Strengthens tolerance, tact and forbearance.
4	Green	Gabriel	Hope	Immaculate Conception, Resurrection	Inspires and gives hope to those who seek to bring forth their creative visions: emphasizes purity, clarity of action, and humility.
5	Orange	Raphael	Mary	Scientific attributes of laws of creation, concentration, listening vocations. Angel of Consecration.	Overseer of those in the field of healing. Guides you in the process of surrendering to your highest good, the rewards of selfless service, and matters of the heart.
6	Indigo	Uriel	Donna Grace	Devotion, Forgiveness, Idealism	Helps attain peace and tranquility. Brings your emotional nature into harmony with Spirit.
7	Violet	Zadkiel	Amethyst	Freedom, Redemption, Transformation	Bearers of the Violet flame. Enhances your Invocations, magnifies the flame of purification and forgiveness as you seek to release all that is not in harmony with Spirit and your highest good.

* Additional information can be found on pages 293-300 of The Golden Promise, by Ronna Herman.

49. The Five Higher Galactic Rays*
(Infused with the Luminescence of the Christ Light)

Ray	Color	Crystal	Esoteric Function**	Exoteric Function***
8	Aquamarine (Seafoam Green with tinge of Violet)	Aquamarine Amethyst Rainbow Flourite	Brings Clarity	Cleanses 4 lower body systems
9	Turquoise Magenta	Turquoise Garnet	Anchors the new Heart/Thymus Chakra	Activates the new life-extending Heart/ Throat Chakra
10	Pearlescent White/Gold	Opal Moonstone	Accesses Golden Richness of Creator	Anchors Light Body, Taps into Eternal Peace and Joy of Creator
11	Iridescent Peach tinged with Gold	Rose Quartz Citrine Pink Tourmaline	Bridge to Causal Mind	Connects you to your Divine I Am Presence
12	Opalescent Gold	Fire Opal	Combination of all other Rays	Activates Christ Consciousness on Earth

* Additional information can be found on pages 255-261 of The Golden Promise, by Ronna Herman.
** Esoteric: the inner, spiritual plane, 4th dimension and above
*** Exoteric: the external, material plane, 3D

Chart created for Ronna by Susan McMann, M.A.

Ronna Herman *STAR QUEST* 6005 Clear Creek Drive, Reno, NV 89502
(702) 856-3654 E-Mail: ronnastar@earthlink.net Website: www.ronnastar.com

ABOUT THE AUTHOR

Ronna Herman is internationally known as a channel for Archangel Michael. His messages of hope and inspiration through Ronna have been featured in more than a dozen New Age and spiritual publications around the world, and translated into most major languages.

A retired business executive and real estate broker, Ronna provides a common sense approach to metaphysics. Her spiritual search began in 1970, and after much intense study and training, she began a second career as a spiritual teacher and counselor. In 1994 she founded StarQuest (www.ronnastar.com).

Ronna has appeared on numerous radio and TV shows, and has spoken twice at the United Nations' S.E.A.T. (The Society for Enlightenment and Transformation). She presents seminars throughout the United States and the world, touching peoples' hearts and connecting them with their soul-self. Those who attend her powerful seminars receive valuable tools to move them to the next level of their spiritual growth.

In her first book, *On Wings of Light,* Ronna shares inspirational messages from Archangel Michael. The book, published in five languages, is a best seller in The Netherlands. Following on this success, Ronna has written a trilogy of six stories that she calls "metafiction." Offered now in manuscript form, the stories in *Once Upon a New World* are based in part on glimpses and remembrances of some of Ronna's past lives and some of her current incarnation experiences.

Ronna lives with her husband, Kent, a retired airline executive, in the high desert country outside Reno, Nevada. When not traveling, Ronna and Kent enjoy gardening and spending time with their combined families consisting of 7 children, 19 grandchildren and 4 great-grandchildren.

Other Books from Mt. Shasta Light Publishing

Calling All Angels — by Christine Chalenor

This beautiful hardcover book was created to share an almost-lost secret. Angels are here, and always have been, and we were always meant to communicate with them. *Calling All Angels* includes the Sacred Covenant treasured by the early Essenes—God's specific instructions on how, when and why to commune with the Angels. Also included are their original morning and evening prayer rituals.

In Part One, you will read about Christine's first dramatic experience with her own Guardian Angel as a small child, and how it became the beginning of a life-long relationship with the Angels. Part Two imparts the ancient, time-tested, but little-known Essene information about communicating daily with the Angels. Part Three consists of prayers invoking the Angels and asking for their assistance with the varied issues and challenges of our lives. There are prayers for children, for healing, for love, for protection, for conflict, for divine guidance, for wisdom, and many others. Open your world to include the Angels, and watch the magic unfold!

The book also includes eleven magnificent color pictures by visionary artist Cheryl Yambrach Rose. She terms her work "art through the eyes of the soul." Cheryl's artwork has graced the covers of books, magazines, calendars, posters, cards and CDs in the U.S., Australia and Europe.

ANGELO'S MESSAGE — BY AURELIA LOUISE JONES

Angelo, the Angel Cat, speaks on behalf of all beings of the Animal Kingdom to all people on this planet. Open your heart to listen and learn from the animals' viewpoint. Angelo will touch your heart with the understanding that this planet was meant to be shared "equally" by ALL sentient beings living here and that ALL living creatures are loved equally and unconditionally by the Creator of ALL.

A call goes out from the Animal Kingdom pleading for mercy and understanding regarding the suffering and barbarian treatments inflicted upon so many of them. You will learn how animal abuse is adding so much to the needless suffering on Earth. The era of Love, Peace and Prosperity that is now at hand cannot and will not come to pass until all forms of life are sanctified, including the Animal Kingdom.

Every animal comes to Earth with a special purpose given to them by the Creator. Angelo and his friends have much to teach us about assisting them in fulfilling their missions.

Aurelia Louise Jones lives with her cats near Mt. Shasta, California, where they are working to create a more compassionate world. A former nurse, naturopath and homeopath, she has rescued many abandoned and abused animals.

Angelo, the Angel Cat, is a sweet and handsome bluepoint Balinese, who has come directly from the angelic realm of cats as a messenger on behalf of the Animal Kingdom.

TELOS — BY DIANNE ROBBINS

Telos is an ancient Lemurian City of Light that exists underneath Mt. Shasta, California. As the Lemurians raised their consciousness to let go of all violence and negativity, they created Heaven on Earth for themselves in their underground cities and also throughout the Hollow Earth. They are looking forward to coming out, when we are ready, to teach us how to do the same here on the surface.

Learn about the wonders awating us when we turn to love.

Mt. Shasta Light Publishing
P. O. Box 1509
Mt. Shasta, CA 96067-1509
USA

Web site: **www.mslpublishing.com**
Email: aurelia@mslpublishing.com
Phone: 530.926.4599
Fax: 530.926.4159

	Price	Qty	Totals
Calling All Angels — (Christine Chalenor)	22.00	___	______
Angelo's Message — (Aurelia Louise Jones)	8.00	___	______
TELOS — (Dianne Robbins)	15.00	___	______
SUBTOTAL			______
7% Sales Tax for CA orders			______
Shipping (see table at left)			______
TOTAL			______

U.S.	$4 + $2 each add'l
Canada	$5 + $3 each add'l
Overseas	$10 + $5 each add'l

Send check or money order payable in U.S. Funds, or charge to (check one): VISA__ MasterCard__ AMEX__ Discover__

Card Number______________________________ Exp.________

Name:____

Address:____

City:__________________________ St:_____ Zip:__________

Phone:_______________ Email:__________________________

Books and Tapes by Ronna Herman

On Wings of Light

Ronna's first book of channelled messages from Archangel Michael is about hope and love: love of self, love of life and how to enjoy the experience of being an empowered spiritual human being. Archangel Michael is made real on the book's pages so that readers feel a tangible connection with his energy, his wisdom and his love.

The messages in this book are positive and life changing. They help us understand who we REALLY are and how to create our perfect realities. Archangel Michael explains why we are here on planet earth and how to be the masters we are in these physical forms.

The Golden Promise

Further messages from Archangel Michael, providing many exercises, meditations, and affirmations to help us release old, self-sabotaging beliefs, and to replace them with empowering, life-changing thought patterns.

If you are ready for the next steps in your spiritual growth, this is the book for you. Many of the principles in the book are also incorporated in the series of I AM Mastery classes Ronna now offers in person and by mail.

***Once Upon a New World** — A Trilogy*

Ronna calls this series of stories "metafiction," since although they are fiction, they are intertwined with a higher truth. They are based on glimpses and remembrances of some of Ronna's past lives, and partially, too, on some of her experiences during the present incarnation. The trilogy is about the journey (incarnations) of one SPARK of the God Force, and Its evolution through time and space. It is an adventure story of love, hope and inspiration.

These stories give new meaning to why we are here on planet earth and where we are going. They teach, in simple language, the Universal Laws and higher truths that are so important to understand and apply masterfully during these times of great change. There are two stories per book.

The Maui Tapes

Contain all the exercises, lectures, meditations and messages from Archangel Michael given at the two-day Harmonic Convergence Anniversary Seminar.

TAPE 1: Brain Waves; Kinesiology; Sacred Breath Toning, Gift of Angelic Helpers; Side B: Meditation: Balancing Chakras; Harmonizing & Balancing Physical, Mental & Emotional Bodies; Connecting with Higher Self · **TAPE 2:** Encode Finger Responses from Higher Self; Break Agreements; Galactic Center Info; Side B: Chakra Center Chants; Language of Light; Universal Laws of Manifestation · **TAPE 3:** Transformational Sacred Breath; Meditation: Clearing Past Lives & Experiencing Reintegration with Divine Self; Side B: Toning with Mudras to Balance the Chakra System & Integrate Higher Frequencies of Light **TAPE 4:** Meditation: Activate & Integrate Five Higher Ray Energies; Build Sanctuary; Commune with Masters & Angelic Helpers; Dropping Into the Alpha State; Side B: Message from Archangel Michael **TAPE 5:** First Ray of Divine Power & Will; Humanity's Descent to Earth; Angelic Origins; Side B: Archangel Michael's Message; Initiation

I AM Mastery Course Tapes

The I AM MASTERY TAPES are support material for the I AM MASTERY PRINTED COURSE—they give an overview and meditation for each chakra, but do not give the full course information.

Tape 99-2: I AM Mastery Course Overview
Side B: Meditation; Class 1: Root Chakra, Red Energy
Tape 99-3: Class 2: 2nd Chakra, Orange Energy, with Meditation
Side B: Class 3: 3rd Chakra, Yellow Energy with Meditation
Tape 99-4: Class 4: 4th Chakra, Green Energy
Side B: Meditation and Message from Archangel Michael
Tape 99-5/6: Class 5: 5th Chakra, Blue Energy with Meditation
Side B: Class 6: 6th Chakra, Indigo Energy, with Meditation
Tape 99-7: Class 7: 7th Chakra, Violet Energy, with Meditation
Tape 99-8: Class 8: Initiation, Overview of 5 Higher Galactic Chakras, Vision for the New Millennium, Message from Archangel Michael

I AM Mastery Meditations (2K-6)

Archangel Michael Messages: Our Lemurian History, Lake Tahoe and Pyramid Lake, Inter-Dimensional Portal Opening and Energy Activation at Grimes Point, Nevada (2K8-T)

ORDER FORM

StarQuest, 6005 Clear Creek Dr., Reno, NV 89502 USA
Phone/Fax: 775.856.3654 Email: ronnastar@earthlink.net
Order online: www.ronnastar.com

	Price	Qty	Totals
On Wings of Light	20.00	___	______
The Golden Promise	23.00	___	______
Once Upon a New World — Books 1,2 & 3			
Manuscripts available prior to publication	CALL	___	______
The Maui Tapes			
Tape 1	11.00	___	______
Tape 2	11.00	___	______
Tape 3	11.00	___	______
Tape 4	11.00	___	______
Tape 5	11.00	___	______
Complete set of five tapes	50.00	___	______
I AM Mastery Course — 8 Lessons			
Printed materials	55.00	___	______
Tape 99-2	12.00	___	______
Tape 99-3	12.00	___	______
Tape 99-4	12.00	___	______
Tape 99-5/6	12.00	___	______
Tape 99-7	12.00	___	______
Tape 99-8	12.00	___	______
Complete set of six tapes	65.00	___	______
I AM Mastery Meditations — Tape 2K-6	12.00	___	______
Our Lemurian History, Lake Tahoe, Pyramid Lake and Grimes Point — Tape 2K8-T	12.00	___	______
SUBTOTAL BOOKS & TAPES			______
Sales Tax of 7.25% for NV shipments			______
Shipping Charges (see table below)			______
TOTAL			______

	Tapes	Books
U.S.	$2 + $.50 each add'l	$4 + $2 each add'l
Canada	$2 + $1 each add'l	$5 + $3 each add'l
Overseas	$2 + $1 each add'l	$10 + $5 each add'l

Send check or money order payable in U.S. Funds, or charge to (check one): VISA__ MasterCard__ AMEX__ Discover__

Card Number________________________________ Exp.________

Name:____

Address:____

City:______________________________ St:_____ Zip:___________

Phone:________________ Email:________________________